MW01193783

What radio hosts in tl
are saying about Michelle Payton's work:

"I enjoyed your (*Birth Mix Patterns*) books. I started with Numerology when I began doing readings more than 35 years ago, but this gives a wonderful and intriguing twist to it all. Amazingly insightful and accurate."

—Ted Andrews, award-winning author of over 40 books and products including *Animal-Speak* and *Nature-Speak*

"Michelle Payton was an awesome guest. Loaded with armfuls of knowledge and wisdom, she came prepared to inform and entertain, and was a smashing success at both."

—Bill Shields, Host *In the Dark*, KBAR Radio, 1230 AM, ID

"Michelle was well informed and entertaining. It's obvious she enjoys her work."   —Ben Williams, Host of *Partyline*, WILO Radio, 1570 AM, IN

"Michelle has an engaging personality and has a gift for insight. She's a wonderful guest."

—Curtis Cheatham, Co-Host WGHT AM Radio *Morning Show*, NJ

"...funny, topical, interesting... the interview will be the talk of the water cooler..."   —Stacy Sturm, *Brad and Stacy in the Morning* on Y93 FM, ND

"Michelle Payton was 'spot on' according to a caller in Australia! Listener feedback was very positive during and after the show. She was a great guest and we look forward to having her back."

—Rob McConnell, host & executive producer, *The "X" Zone* Radio Show, Ontario (Canada)

Birth Mix Patterns

and Loving Relationships
using Astrology, Numerology,
and Birth Order

Birth Mix Patterns

and Loving Relationships using Astrology, Numerology, and Birth Order

M. A. Payton

Award-winning Author of
Adventures of a Mainstream Metaphysical Mom,
"Soul"utions, and the *Birth Mix Patterns* series

The Left Side
Powell, Ohio

Interior body text is set in 12 point Centar by Pete Masterson, Æonix
Publishing Group, www.aeonix.com
Cover illustration by Prescott Hill

ISBN-10: 0-9719804-4-6
ISBN-13: 978-0-9719804-4-0
LCCN: 2007925180

Published by
The Left Side
437 Hopewell Drive
Powell, Ohio 43065

Phone: 614-785-9821
Fax: 614-785-9819
www.theleftside.com

Printed in the United States of America

Contents

I. What If You Knew You Were OK?

I Love Me

A woman who read one of my books in the *Birth Mix Patterns* series wrote me with a question on a Pisces love interest from decades ago (among other details). At one point in my communication I wrote (completely unaware of her experience), "Being Pisces... this sign can have challenges grounding in the physical... they are (generally) very much in-the-moment so when someone tells a Pisces to meet at a specific place in the future (maybe in a couple of days, for instance) they may or may not make that appointment when in a less grounded state. Some perceive this as having difficulty with commitment, focus, or even being disrespectful. My perception is the Pisces doesn't skip appointments (for instance) to make others upset or to be disrespectful, they simply have another world/reality to explore in-the-moment. It turns out her heart was broken when this love interest didn't show up for a date they had made in high school nearly 40 years ago. As a result of this one incident, she felt this was all about her, was her fault, that there was something wrong with her.

On the flip side, there are those that think that "it's" everyone else's fault. For instance, one of my children said to me, "Mom, you're making me mad." My response was, "No, you're making yourself mad. That is your choice." We all have choices about the emotions, judgments, and opinions we own, wear, and demonstrate. Many of the emotions we form involve people (including the evaluation of ourselves).

So these examples set the tone. Regardless of who you are, being in more predictable situations creates trust. From trusting that your refrigerator works and your vehicle will start, to trusting that relationships work, this type of confidence then creates soul-based labels like comfort, gratitude, joy, and love. By the time you've finished this book you will trust what is right about you, and everyone else for that matter, utilizing the Birth Mix Patterns process. You will be walking down the path of "I Love Me." Even in dysfunction, when having an understanding of habits in connection with BMP, we can find ways to turn situations and relationships into functional. To clarify further, this is not a book of making excuses for your Birth Mix, nor is it a psychiatric evaluation. But it is about acknowledging and understanding your and others' patterns through an alternative method (if you choose to), and deciding how you will allow this to guide you down your happy, peaceful, graceful, contented path.

In this book (like the first two Birth Mix Pattern books) you will see analysis on many famous people but with an emphasis on love relationships. I've developed a snapshot chart that will help you read, understand, and lay-out your own and others' Birth Mix Patterns information quickly. You'll notice that I have given each of the Astrology, Numerology Life Path and Sub-lessons, and Birth Order title descriptors to aid in your quick, top-line understanding. And I've also introduced the concept of masculine/yang and feminine/ying to the personalities. A note to enthusiasts, this is not based on how Astrology defines masculine and feminine. From an emotional stand-point, yang is loud, masculine, aggressive, heavy, rough. Ying is soft, feminine, gently assertive, light.

When we go through the many case histories, allow yourself to think intuitively about what a humanitarian, a leader, an intuitive, someone who is a builder of order, life partaker, etc. might do. Notice also how the traits change in a mix because they balance, accelerate, and/or deflate certain dispositions. It will be helpful to go to my website, www.MichellePayton.com, from time to time to see text and hear audio examples from my numerous radio appearances and recorded seminars to brush up on new concepts, and get a feel for how this all comes together live.

We all learn differently. Some like to read the case histories first then study the Birth Mix Patterns details. Others like to first study the BMP details. Regardless of your style, I suggest all of you go to sections IV and V before you do either of the above, and calculate your specific Numerology, Sun Sign and Birth Order. If you have a love relationship, do that BMP as well. Write your information on a piece of paper, fold it (if necessary) and use it as a bookmark. Every time you come across a personality that has similar qualities to your BMP calculations it will become a part of your consciousness.

Remember that you have a handle on how personalities come together as a daily observer. I've done a number of workshops and telephone seminars with detailed personalities that add, embellish, and revise my study guides because of their extensive study in one or more areas in Birth Mix Patterns. When reading this book, allow yourself to be an expert—add, delete, embellish, and revise titles and text to my descriptions.

Whatever you need to do to create communication experiences that result in more peace, love, honor, respect, truth, grace, and elegance for yourself and others, do it!

The *Birth Mix Patterns* Series

The Birth Mix Patterns process was created for people who have an interest in Astrology, Numerology, and Birth Order, but aren't interested in learning all the technical "ins and outs" all of these subjects. Those experienced in one of the BMP areas are interested in being introduced to how the other dimensions fit together. Still more experienced astrologers, and numerologists enjoy reading this series because "it gives a wonderful and intriguing twist to it all" —Ted Andrews, award-winning author of *Animal-Speak*, and *Nature-Speak*. Wherever you fit, the information is presented in a way that helps you understand how it applies to real people.

This is the third book in the *Birth Mix Patterns* series. In each book I introduce new concepts, in addition to Birth Mix Patterns, to increase the understanding and completeness of how personalities are impacted and interpreted. While there are so many points that could be made when looking at Numerology, Astrology, and Birth Order, I intentionally provide information that you can easily calculate and apply within hours of reading this book.

Again, we all learn in different ways and have different levels of understanding of Astrology, Numerology, Birth Order, Conscious Living, and New Age concepts. For a more thorough understanding of learning about people and how Astrology, Numerology and Birth Order have impacted people all over the world, here's a bit more information on what you will find in the two previous *Birth Mix Patterns* instruction books.

In *Birth Mix Patterns: Astrology, Numerology, and Birth Order, and their effects on the Past, Present and Future* my emphasis is on chronologically introducing Life Path: 1, 2, 3, 4 and so on, Astrology Sun Sign: Aries, Taurus, Gemini and so on, Birth Order: First Born, Middle, and so on. This book was conceived a year after "*SOUL'utions* where I introduced Financial, Intellectual, Physical, Social, and Spiritual Balance with Soul which included structured goal setting processes and exercises and utilized Numerology to get to know yourself and others a bit better. FIPSS (an acronym for the above-mentioned areas of life) was fresh in my mind when I wrote the first book in the BMP series. So in the chronological listing of 1, 2, 3, Aries, Taurus, First Born, Middle, etc., I also included how all are impacted in their financial, intellectual, physical, social, and spiritual lives. It analyzes all the U.S. Presidents and First Ladies through Bush of 2000, and many other historical figures. You are also introduced to Personal Years using Numerology, and how Earth Cycles (changing of the seasons) impact our daily lives.

In *Birth Mix Patterns: Astrology, Numerology, and Birth Order, and their effects on Families and Other Groups that Matter* my emphasis was on providing historical information on groups and individuals that made up the groups then demonstrated how each individual Life Path 1, 2, 3, 4, Astrology Sun Sign Aries, Taurus, Gemini, Birth Order First Born, Middle mingled. I introduced ideas on how to further understand the energy of the group by analyzing the date of establishment (official date group was "born" or "reborn"). You also get a peek at how to determine basic personality patterns without a birth date.

The Benefits of Fully Expressing Your Birth Mix

When doing Birth Mix Patterns analysis there is a functional (having a good day), dysfunctional (having a bad day), and an "I have no idea who I am" expression (which could result in both functional and dysfunctional patterns). For instance, I did an event for *Elle Magazine* at a major car show. I, literally, did nearly 100 (5 minute) readings that day and people were amazed at how accurate their quick sessions were. Even the Vice President of the major sponsoring car company came to the *Elle* booth to meet me, shook my hand, and said I was the talk of the event (and remember this was a car show).

I mention this because I generally give the functional explanation with gentle nudges of "you might want to think about..." when I'm doing quick radio and other promotional readings. I have had the opportunity to speak with thousands of people, and the majority of the time the information that I share is spot on. There are two reasons for this success: Simply the study of an already accurate system of Astrology, Numerology, Birth Order, and the second key to clarity is the observation of how the three dimensions of information combine, accelerate, decelerate, and/or neutralize each other. So back to my story, out of the over eight hours of readings that I did, I caught a man out of the corner of my eye, in line, whose vibe seemed off balance. When it was finally his chance to get a quick reading he said, "That doesn't sound a bit like me." I wasn't surprised, nor taken back. It required more time to give him an in-depth assessment, taking it past gentle nudges and into comparisons of functional and dysfunctional patterns.

The point is if you aren't able to fully express your BMP functionally, and/or lack clarity as to what that is (your cosmic purpose, in essence), then you will be off-center. Awareness opens doors.

That being said, nothing rules you. You are the master of choice. And this process doesn't resonate for everyone.

So let's get started on Love Relationships when working with Birth Mix Patterns, and you be the judge.

II. Birth Mix Patterns Case Studies

The Beautiful People:

Acting must be a burning passion for those who have chosen this as a career. On one side of the spectrum, is it worth all the personal invasions, the lengthy travel, separation from family and friends, accurate and inaccurate observations and reports? On the other side, for some, the attention, the travel, etc., are part of the perks. But, then pondering, aren't we all day-to-day actors on a stage? We have many scenes, dramas, costume changes, and a variety of roles that we play. So how do we get the script to know who we are talking to, how to dress, what to say, when and how to say it? Let's take a look at Birth Mix Patterns as one option to getting the life script.

I Love Lucy—Lucille Ball & Desi Arnaz

Their story: Desi was Cuban-American. He was born to a wealthy family that also held political office. When revolution in Cuba reared its ugly head, he and his family fled to Miami, Florida. Penniless, his family worked odd jobs to survive. Desi pursued a career in music and became all the rage when he introduced the conga line and his hit *Babalu*. He then transitioned to movies, and eventually created and produced the classic sitcom *I Love Lucy* through a production company, Desilu, that both he and Lucy owned. Arnaz was not originally slotted to be Lucy's (Lucille Ball) television husband, but she insisted that he play her on-air spouse so they could spend more time together. They both insisted on good taste that avoided racial, ethnic, and handicapped jokes. In addition, Arnaz was very thankful to be in America. Through the show (that ran six years), he demonstrated humble beginnings to complete success—The American Dream. Lucille Ball did not have the same immediate success as Arnaz. For the first ten years of her career she was hired and fired, and experienced moderate successes in "B" movies. Even with *I Love Lucy* they had to go on vaudeville (an entertainment road show that had many small skits and usually one headline show) to prove to the CBS network that this would be a hit. Lucille Ball would eventually earn the title the "Queen of Comedy." Their relationship, however, was said to be volatile, and arguments revolved around Desi's indiscretions, particularly with other women. They eventually divorced in 1960, but remained friends until his death.

Here's a BMP snapshot chart for Lucille Ball and Desi Arnaz:

	LUCILLE BALL	DESI ARNAZ
Birth date	Aug. 6, 1911	Mar. 2, 1917
Life Path #	17/8-Physical Manifester	14/5- Unending Talent
Astrology Sun	Leo-Leader	Pisces-Intuitive
Major Sub-lesson #	6-Server/Responsible One	2-Inward Creator
Minor Sub-lesson #	6-Server/Responsible One	2-Inward Creator
Birth Order	First Born Girl (one younger brother)	Unknown

Acceleration Points	This is a very generous BMP. Leo, 6 loves to serve a defined community. And with the 8, 6, and Leo this could also mean over-caring through money. To this mix it is very important to not enable through over-helping. Her ability to lead was accelerated as well with the First Born and Leo influences.	This is a much more inward BMP with Pisces, and 2 processing. The 5 would create a great deal of talent. The result would likely be inward processing with a lot of internal chatter (due to constantly creating).

LUCILLE BALL BMP SUMMARY:

Lucille's mix is that of a very generous person that would enjoy serving a community. Her Leo leader, 6 responsible one is the community server that would be very protective of her defined inner circle. Her circle could be defined as her fans, her biological family, or her employees, for instance. She may have over-delivered for people and caused herself some stress and resentment at times. This mix may train people (unknowingly) to depend on them too much. Her 8 physical manifester Life Path would enable her to make money, have vision to succeed in business, but would require focus to maintain wealth. Money always shows up for 8's, but they don't always know how to manage it because they can take it for granted. With her 8, First Born, and Leo influences, leading and managing would be natural for her. She was one of only two women in the entertainment world of her time who owned a production studio. Her masculine/yang traits are Leo, 8, and First Born. Her more feminine/ying is 6.

DESI ARNAZ BMP SUMMARY:

Desi had a very ying mix. This would be very attractive for the opposite gender as he would be a sensitive (interpreted as), caring guy with his Pisces intuitive, 2 inward creator mix. His life is actually quite amazing as he, literally, went from riches to rags to riches. Within only a few years of coming to America he made a name for himself in music, in acting, and then in television production. His 5 unending talent Life Path would attribute to his success in multi-tasking (I consider this more yang because it can be so noisy with lots of multi-tasking)—acting, music, production, and womanizing.

LUCILLE BALL & DESI ARNAZ BMP SUMMARY:

Lucille's more aggressive approach to success as Leo, First Born, with 8 and 6 influences certainly earned her the title of "Queen of the 'B's" (meaning Queen of "B" movies in her early days), and "Queen of Comedy" as her career progressed. The comedy comes from her caregiver side as a 6 cosmic mother role and Leo interest in overseeing a community (to keep them happy). To keep Desi and Lucy's relationship intact, she insisted that Desi be her on-air husband in *I Love Lucy*. She didn't take no for an answer when CBS thought that the American public would not accept a Cuban-American and a redhead as a married couple, and demonstrated this by going on the road to promote the show (in vaudeville) demonstrating that "the people" approved.

Lucy's persistence wasn't enough, however, when it came to other women. Desi was creative in many areas (5), could read people and situations quickly (Pisces), knew the value of listening (2), was handsome, and had a charming accent. Women were one of his vices that led to their marriage demise. It was clear that they never stopped loving each other as they talked regularly until his death.

Now let's go from the Queen of Comedy to the Queen of Egypt. Well, at least in the movies.

20ᵀᴴ Century Cleopatra & Marc Antony Love— Elizabeth Taylor & Richard Burton

Their story: Elizabeth, born in England to American parents, played many classic roles from an early age of nine in films. She was said to be the highest paid actress of her time and is an Academy Award winner. In addition to her professional accomplishments, she is involved in a number of charitable organizations. Burton, of Welsh heritage, was known for his distinct voice, was a classic actor in films and, said to be the greatest British actor ever, was nominated for many Academy Awards as well. They met and fell in love when working on the set of *Cleopatra*. Elizabeth Taylor has been married eight times to seven separate men (her first marriage was right after she graduated high school at age 18). Remember this is Hollywood—the land of "who's doin' who." While I have not interviewed Elizabeth, maybe she believes marriage was a connection that had to be made in order to experience true intimacy (instead of moving from bed to bed). Richard Burton was quoted as saying: "You'd be surprised at the morals of many women stars that are regarded by the public as goody-two-shoes. They leap into bed with any male in grabbing distance. That's what makes me mad when I read stuff hinting Liz is a scarlet woman because she's been married five times. She's only had five men in her life whereas those goody-two-shoes have lost count." (from the book *Who's Afraid of Elizabeth Taylor?* written by Brenda Maddox). So, instead of looking at all her marriages, I thought I'd look at the most special one with Richard Burton. Why is this so special? Richard Burton was the man she partnered with the longest (more than ten years), and he was the only man she married twice.

Here's a BMP snapshot chart for Elizabeth Taylor and Richard Burton:

	ELIZABETH TAYLOR	RICHARD BURTON
Birth date	Feb. 27, 1932	Nov. 10, 1945
Life Path #	17/8-Physical Manifester	13/4- Builder of Order
Astrology Sun	Pisces-Intuitive	Scorpio-Patient Achiever
Major Sub-lesson #	9-Humanitarian	1-Leader
Minor Sub-lesson #	2-Inward Creator & 7-Source of Knowledge	1 with 0-Accelerated Leader
Birth Order	First Born Girl (one older brother)	Unknown (reports of many brothers and sisters)
Acceleration Points	This is a very balanced BMP. While 8 is yang, Pisces is more ying. While 9 is more ying, 7 is more yang. They have various weights but would still be in balance.	Things would have to be done in very specific ways with a 4 process-oriented, and strategic thinking Scorpio. With the 10 for the day of birth, this is an accelerated leader, listening would not have been one of his strengths (unless he consciously developed this). As a special note—his year is a 1, day 1, month double 1. Passion to achieve would have been very high (Scorpio, and accelerated 1's). This is a very masculine, yang mix.

Here's how their information fits together.

ELIZABETH TAYLOR BMP SUMMARY:

Elizabeth is the classic 8 physical manifester. She was one of the top paid women actresses of her time, and has won numerous awards and recognitions over her many years as an actress. While at the same time, she has the Pisces way of being able to read people and situations quickly (not all people, of course, but many). Her 9 major humanitarian influence has driven her to support a number of causes. She has minor influences balance with a ying 2 inward creator, yang 7 analyzer (inward but a bit more yang/masculine). So while she creates, intuits, supports charity, she still has that ability to physically manifest and analyze to get to the best result.

Richard Burton's BMP Summary:

The best way to describe this mix is internally loud, yang/masculine. This description can be deceiving because loud doesn't always mean words. It could mean stubborn, burning internal passion, loud inner voice, etc. As a Life Path 4, Scorpio, accelerated 1 (with the 0 it doubles the intensity), Burton's mix would create method, keep it Scorpio quiet until completion, then would tell all the "players" what roles they were to take on as a result of his thought process. With the double leader number (10), it may have been difficult for him to listen at times, especially when he was building more order. His Birth Order was not available, but if he was First Born or Only, this would have created an even bigger need to control situations, and people.

Elizabeth Taylor's & Richard Burton's BMP Summary:

Elizabeth has a feminine and masculine balance that has served her well. She's intuitive, yet analyzes when necessary. She's a physical manifester, yet she is a humanitarian focusing on those in need. Richard's mix is more methodical, and controlling. He has a major theme of control with his double leader and Scorpio influences. As long as Elizabeth's softer qualities were present in their relationship, then balance could be achieved. But if Burton's masculinity and control tendencies became overpowering then the marriage would be out of balance. Dysfunctional traits are, of course, accelerated when alcohol (Burton was known to be a heavy drinker), drugs (Burton was known to be addicted to pain medication for his back pain), stress, and lack of sleep (Burton was an insomniac) enter the picture.

Let's move from a classic English couple to the trendy couple that many in the UK have their eyes on in the 2000's.

SOCCER & SPICE & EVERYTHING NICE
—DAVID BECKHAM & POSH

Their story: My First Born daughter was completely into the *Spice Girls* in the 1990's, an all-female English pop group that introduced the term "Girl Power." Some would say that they are one of the most successful commercial female groups, selling over 120 million records. Their success was so great that Britain was comparing them to the Beatles. Terms like "Spice World," and "Spicemania," were rampant. Posh (real name Victoria Beckham) was the cute, tiny Spice Girl that people would always ask "does she have an eating disorder?" Prior to Spice Girls she was in an unknown/unsigned music group, did various modeling and dancing jobs. Growing up, she lived comfortably.

David Beckham is an English, hunky, famous, professional soccer (football if you are not from the United States) player. He began playing professionally at age 17, was the captain for the English national team for a number of years, has set and broken numerous records in the sport. He is an icon in England.

Put these two together, and the media has gone wild (and they have certainly given them things to write about with their lavish lifestyle).

Both are beautiful, successful, and have kept Britain on the map in soccer (Europe football), and in pop music.

Here's a BMP snapshot chart for Posh and David Beckham:

	POSH	DAVID BECKHAM
Birth date	April 17, 1974	May 2, 1975
Life Path #	15/6-Server	29/11-Intuitive
Astrology Sun	Aries-Charming Leader	Taurus-Stabilizer
Major Sub-lesson #	8-Physical Manifester	2-Inward Creator
Minor Sub-lesson #	1-Leader & 7-Source of Knowledge	2-Inward Creator
Birth Order	First Born Girl (two other sisters)	Unknown
Acceleration Points	This is a yang balanced BMP. 6 Cosmic Mother would be the ying in her mix, the element that softens her.	This is more of an inward, listener, pleaser mix (11, 2, Taurus can be complacent). A ying/feminine mix.

Here's how their information fits together.

POSH'S BMP SUMMARY:

Posh's 8 major sub-lesson is outwardly evident with her lavish lifestyle (similar to Elizabeth Taylor), with international pop figures announced (like Elton John and Elizabeth Hurley) as godparents to her sons. Her media impression (as an outsider like myself looking in) is an intense woman, which makes her curt Aries persona more publicly prominent (minor 7 researcher/loner can accelerate this a bit as well). Her rich and famous lifestyle may be her Aries inspiration point, another inspiration point is likely her music (especially as a *Spice Girl* being a role model to so many young girls). As a Life Path 6, she would experience fulfillment by overseeing a community, helping the community receive attention positively, feeling real love for that community, and she would receive love in return for her generosity (that can be a result of money, time, other). She may over-give to that community, and this can become a resentment point over time. This would be self-inflicted resentment for training people to rely so much on her. She would like how gratitude for her service felt as it would also feed her Aries lead through inspiration need. She has minor influences of yang 1 leader, yang 7 analyzer (inward but a bit more yang/masculine). Being First Born would have a major influence on her expectation to be in control and lead as well. 8, 7, 1, First Born, Aries are more yang/masculine. 6 is more ying/feminine. Because 6 is a higher ranking number/trait in her mix, this would have a tendency to soften her among people she trusts.

DAVID BECKHAM'S BMP SUMMARY:

This is more of a ying mix. Inward processing 2, and 11 are prominent in his mix. The 2 inward creator is a team motivator, and have what seems to be shy tendencies in public (as 2's has a tendency to be listeners more than talkers). The 11 maximizes the journey, and is in-the-moment. I consider this a highly charged 2, with 11 also being a master number. The reason why 11/2 can be good listeners is because they can actually hear past the spoken word—they can feel vibes, sense situations, and lead intuitively. 11's don't always do well in formal education, because they look to life experiences to define their truths. At the same time, with the Taurus energy, this wouldn't mean that Beckham is impulsive. The Taurus looks for stability and security. In fact, one of the ways that Beckham is expressing this is through Obsessive Compulsive Disorder (reported that he has a constant need to have clean and tidy things). Eliminating risk increases security.

POSH & DAVID BECKHAM'S BMP SUMMARY:

When looking at Posh and David as husband and wife, Posh is yang/masculine, and Beckham is ying/feminine. This means that David would express himself more softly, Posh more aggressively, or a bit more vocally. His Taurus matches her 8 major influence when it comes to money. 8 attracts the flow of money, Taurus is a collector and saver of money (adds to security, and comfort). Her Aries (usually a bit more of an outward communicator), and his 11 and 2 inward influences would complement each other. The conflict could come in when she over-communicates (6, Aries, First Born), and he under-communicates (11, Taurus, 2). If they respect one another enough they will learn to strike a Middle ground. The 7 source of knowledge in Posh, while not a major influence, would say that she looks for facts, and may not trust information unless she has been able to look at it closely (not in all things, but specific things important to her). The First Born, 8, Aries, 7 in her may have issues hearing what others have to say. David has a more faith-based mix (not to be confused with religion). Posh's mix doesn't encourage intuitive, faith-based leaps quite as much.

And then there's another icon couple from the late 1960's, Sonny & Cher for the United States.

I GOT YOU BABE—SONNY & CHER

Their story: In the beginning, Sonny was the organizer and go-getter in the relationship. Being eleven years her senior was likely part of this reason (they met when she was just 16 years old), but he also knew the business better than she (at first). Sonny was married, at the time he met Cher at a coffee shop. She was an aspiring singer, Sonny had been a songwriter since the 1950's. He ended his marriage in the 1960's to be with her.

Then professionally, they developed a duo called "Sonny & Cher." They had one daughter, who announced as a adult that she was gay. Cher later went on to have a successful solo career, divorced, and remarried. While Sonny had a great deal of knowledge, there was no Sonny without Cher so he went into the restaurant business, later became the mayor in Palm Springs, CA because he was frustrated with the local bureaucracy, then ran and was elected into congress (in the 1990's). His life came to a shocking end when he died in a skiing accident in the late 1990's.

The success, the independence, the brassiness and free spirit that encompassed Cher is what so many are attracted to. Amazing costumes, trend-setter "up yours" attitude, great voice (selling hundreds of millions of records), and award-winning actress (Academy Award, Oscar, Grammy, Emmy, and Golden Globes winner), and mult-million heiress, Cher has it all.

Here's Sonny & Cher's BMP snapshot chart:

	SONNY	CHER
Birth date	Feb. 16, 1935	May 20, 1946
Life Path #	18/9-Humanitarian	9-Humanitarian
Astrology Sun	Aquarius-Out-of-the-Box	Taurus-Stabilizer
Major Sub-lesson #	7-Source of Knowledge	2-Inward Creator (accelerated with 0)
Minor Sub-lesson #	1-Leader & 6-Server	2-Inward Creator
Birth Order	Unknown	Unknown (half sister, age difference unknown)

Acceleration Points	9, Aquarius would create a social, people person. 6 and 9 would make for one interested in being a strong supporter of community to help others (create perfect world).	2 accelerated with 0 is an inward creator. 9 and Taurus would say she is a people pleaser, and would be highly interested in humane issues. People's dramas and being taken advantage of are likely if unaware of this pattern.

CHER'S **BMP** SUMMARY:

Cher was said to be a bit shy as a younger woman, and had problems with being nervous on-stage. This is because her 2 and Taurus are more subdued and modest. She's more the listener, supporter, team motivator, preferring to be safe and secure (many times means being with more familiar people). Her 9 and Taurus would point to her interest in helping others, wanting to make the world a better place, making it safe and secure for everyone. She has a Cher Charitable Foundation that gives money to charities and causes that touch her heart. The Taurus, 9 and 2 (with accelerated 0) points to a person that has the capability of being open-minded and supporting diversity. It's interesting that the amazing costumes she wears are not indicative of her mix. But, as I understand it, she did this (at least, at first), to calm her nerves when on stage. So that she didn't have to use as many words (her 2ness), maybe the clothing spoke louder than words. Her eyes are the windows to her soul. They always seem relaxed and/or amused (Taurus, 2, 9 like). Her mix is completely ying/feminine, unless she is an Only or First Born.

Sonny's BMP Summary:

A 9, Aquarian, Sonny would be everybody's friend, but he had the major influence of 7 that made him a source of knowledge. The 7 was the one that knew the value of research and becoming an expert to create success. With his 9, and 6 this would make him a great public servant. The 6 is the most commonly found number amongst U.S. Presidents and First Ladies in the 20 and 21st centuries (see my first *Birth Mix Patterns* book in the series for more information on this). The 9 is one who looks for a better world, and is very compassionate. It's no wonder Sonny was compelled to go into politics. His yang/masculine 7 (Birth Order unknown) drove him to measurable success. All other traits are more ying/feminine.

Sonny & Cher's BMP Summary:

Both Sonny and Cher were Life Path 9's. They would be a kind, compassionate couple with interests in healing the world. Sonny as an Aquarian, and Cher a Taurus, created a very sociable, likeable pair. When they met, the attraction would likely have been that they had a lot of fun together. They were likely great friends as much as lovers. What put Sonny in the lead role was his 6 responsible one (also called server), his 7 analyzer, and the fact that he was more than a decade older than Cher with experience in the music business. Being a teen-ager, she needed a mentor to make it in the business to which she aspired. It would have been very easy for her to put Sonny on a pedestal with the number of things that they had in common, plus the "go-getter" traits that she hadn't yet developed.

In the entertainment world, Cher will always be admired for her out-of-the-box approach to life, and that doesn't stop with her.

The Hollywood Squares—Brad Pitt, Jennifer Aniston, Angelina Jolie, & Vince Vaughn

Their stories: Okay, pay close attention. The following square (meaning we have four points) is full of beautiful people with Brad Pitt (seemingly) being the prize. A major motion picture talent, Brad is known to be one of the sexiest men in the early 2000's. Jennifer Aniston is the first wife of Brad Pitt. She is a television talent, known best for her role as "Rachel" in the popular sitcom *Friends*, winning an Emmy Award and Golden Globe for her work. By 2006, she successfully transitioned to major motion pictures working alongside many accomplished actors.

Angelina Jolie has been said to be one of the most beautiful women in the world, with her physical trade-mark (among others) being her full lips. She is a major motion picture star known also for her action hero roles (for younger audiences) in *Tomb Raider* as Lara Croft, but has also done many classic films as well that have resulted in professional recognition, including an Academy Award. We've watched her grow (through the media, and her film roles) from rebel to swan. She has served as a role model to her professional peers, as well as the world as a goodwill ambassador for the United Nations. Angelina is the second wife of Brad Pitt, mother to his first biological child, and they adopted two children together (which received a great deal of publicity with their origins from Ethiopia and Cambodia).

And then there is Vince Vaughn, known for his comedian roles in motion pictures. He became a love interest of Jennifer's following her highly publicized break-up, and divorce. The reason for the big scandal? Brad Pitt and Angelina Jolie did a movie together called *Mr. and Mrs. Smith*, and were attracted to each other while Brad was still married to Jennifer. Rumors flew, and tabloids buzzed as a whirlwind separation in January

2005 and final divorce in October 2005 became public. Brad Pitt adopted Angelina's two children by December 2005, Angelina confirmed she was pregnant with Brad's child in January 2006, and then they were married within the year.

So returning to the late 1990's to early 2000's there was a hot couple that many put on the Hollywood pedestal as a great, grounded couple. It was Brad Pitt and Jennifer Aniston. As a couple they were very private about their personal lives.

Here's a BMP snapshot chart of Brad and Jennifer:

	BRAD PITT	JENNIFER ANISTON
Birth date	Dec. 18, 1963	Feb. 11, 1969
Life Path #	13/4-Builder of Order	20/2- Inward Creator
Astrology Sun	Sagittarius-Life Partaker	Aquarius-Out-of-the-Box
Major Sub-lesson #	9-Humanitarian	11/2-Intuitive, In-the-moment
Minor Sub-lesson #	1-Leader & 8-Physical Manifester	11, 1 & 1, Intuitive Leader
Birth Order	First Born of 3 (one brother, one sister)	First Born Girl (reports of three brothers)
Acceleration Points	4 & 9 mix creates "letting go" issues with people and processes. 9 & Sag mix creates love for people, great networker, loving events/gatherings/parties, and esoteric conversations. As a First Born child this would accelerate process creation needs to control situations.	2 accelerated with 0, 11/2, Aquarius shows very private, inward creator, and thinker. Can be fun and social but will be overloaded with too many people in a mix. She has superior listening, intuitive skills.

BRAD PITT **BMP** SUMMARY:

As a Life Path 4, Brad may be more of a hands-on, process-oriented person. Like all of us, our strengths are our weaknesses, and vice versa. So his strength with embracing methods (to create order, decrease chaos) is also his weakness because 4's can become so committed to a process for the sake of process. They can forget why they are following a path in the first place so it would likely take a bit longer to learn certain lessons (having to experience more than a few times). 4's functionally will demonstrate loyalty. 4's dysfunctionally will demonstrate stubbornness because breaking process means that he has to start all over again to redefine a new concept. As First Born boy, this accelerates the 4 need to put processes in place as a control device.

When complimenting the 4 with a 9 major influence, this could lead to over-commitment to relationships and events that are no longer productive for this mix/individual.

The 8 minor sub-influence is the physical manifester and has a strong pull (money, property, business ventures). Because 9 is a higher ranking number in this mix, at some point the humanitarian, less monetary, efforts would be the first priority in life and physical items are second priority. Sagittarians are life partakers, and this creates more pull for the 8 qualities. Sagittarians are also seekers of the more esoteric meaning of life which creates more pull for 9/humanitarian driven by faith, commitment, and compassion (again esoteric). So there are push and pull dynamics—money, better world humanitarian, physical indulgence, spiritual completion.

We've done a few case studies now. If you are having a difficult time grasping the BMP snapshot chart, here is how each trait weighs in visually. Each part of the Birth Mix Patterns segment has an influence on the total personality (this is a specific example for Brad Pitt). The most influential BMP is at the base or foundation of the pyramid (bigger is better in this particular case). The top layer shows the resulting accelerators of all the information building up to it—meaning that Astrology, Numerology, and Birth Order are the foundation pieces that create the peak. So, if words don't work for you as well, create this BMP pyramid in its place when studying yourself and others.

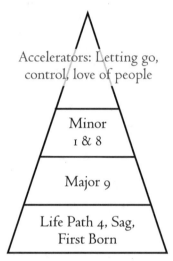

Accelerators: Letting go, control, love of people

Minor
1 & 8

Major 9

Life Path 4, Sag,
First Born

JENNIFER ANISTON **BMP SUMMARY:**

As a Life Path 2, Jennifer would be a great listener, counselor, team motivator. This is a person that looks for that perfect environment, one that nurtures mind, body and spirit. Because this path is not always an overt leader, it can take some time to fully develop her own talents. She would tend to serve others first. This is more of a ying, feminine, soft approach.

Being an Aquarian out-of-the-box thinker, there is a great deal of inward creation as well, and there are times when this Sun Sign would seem a bit removed, or distracted. The Major sub-influence of master number 11 (day of birth) could also be called an 11/2 and is highly intuitive. All these segments are inward processing, very intuitive personality traits. If she is an Only child then this accelerates her need even more to have alone-time processing. With her BMP, protection from large groups that pull too much psychic energy would be essential to keeping her balanced.

Brad Pitt & Jennifer Aniston BMP Summary Mix:

The attraction to Jennifer Aniston is that she is a great supporter, listener, and has vision as a master number 11. The 9 in Brad Pitt's mix reveals his compassionate side. As a Life Path 4, Brad thinks more with his head, is more deliberate, planned, and he might call that being more "realistic." Jennifer would think more creatively in-the-moment, and more intuitively which is opposite to Brad. If they both had an appreciation and respect for opposite thinking processes, then the relationship would continue to flourish.

Brad, as a Sag, would want to go out to events/parties/travel more. Jennifer would be content to be with a smaller, close-knit group of people. This could decrease the fun factor for Brad at times (unless these close-knit friends would be really swinging people). Their relationship lasted (from dating until divorce) about seven years.

Back to their story: Because Brad and Jennifer were a private couple, only their closest friends and family would know the true story of their split-up and ultimate divorce. But, Brad and Angelina did a movie together, following the making of this movie Brad and Jennifer separated then divorced in 2005, Angelina was pregnant with Brad's first child in 2005 (announced in 2006), Brad adopted her two (adopted) children (in 2005), and they were married (in 2006). So why was this relationship so intense so quickly?

Here's a BMP snapshot chart for Brad and Angelina:

	BRAD PITT	**ANGELINA JOLIE**
Birth date	Dec. 18, 1963	June 4, 1975
Life Path #	13/4-Builder of Order	32/5- Unending Talent
Astrology Sun	Sagittarius-Life Partaker	Gemini- Witty Change Agent
Major Sub-lesson #	9-Humanitarian	4-Builder of Order
Minor Sub-lesson #	1-Leader & 8-Physical Manifester	4~Builder of Order
Birth Order	First Born of 3 (one brother, one sister)	First Born girl (one brother)
Acceleration Points	4 & 9 mix creates "letting go" issues with people and processes. 9 & Sag mix creates love for people, great networker, loving events/gatherings/parties, and esoteric conversations. As a First Born child this would accelerate process creation needs to control situations.	5 & Gemini accelerates need for change and new experiences, resulting in sometimes being fickle and easily bored. 4 is her only sub-lesson so she'll have a process builder focus, and as a First Born girl this would accelerate process creation needs to control situations.

ANGELINA JOLIE **BMP SUMMARY:**

As a Life Path 5 and a Gemini, new experiences would be crucial. She would be easily bored, and as a result can be very fickle. Angelina would likely be a master multi-tasker. Good quality completion of projects may be a challenge due to loss of interest, or simply having lots of ideas and not enough time to finish all of them.

With the 4 as a major and minor sub-lesson, Angelina may be more of a hands-on, process-oriented person. Because she has so much change agent energy in her mix, she would likely build a process for others to manage then walk away from the event/person/project to experience the new. As First Born girl, this accelerates the 4 need to put processes in place as a control device.

Brad Pitt & Angelina Jolie BMP Summary:

Angelina's Gemini and 5 mix would give the Sagittarian in Brad Pitt a roller coaster thrill. She is all about change and experiencing new things and this would fill the Sag fun meter. Part of this adventure has come with Angelina's lifestyle, and it being so transparent. She has been very open about her bi-sexuality, and taken a clear position that love is love regardless of gender. A bigger picture commitment, that Angelina has made, is as ambassador to the United Nations. This good work made a major impact on Pitt, increasing his 9 humanitarian commitment to those in need.

They both have major 4 influences. They both appreciate establishing foundation, are hard workers, are organized, and this mix supports that they are realistic, grounded thinkers.

Because they are so similar in many ways, they may accelerate each others' weaknesses of : lacking focus, being too adventurous (5 and Sag), working too hard (4), being too controlling (First Born), and possibly being stubborn (4).

Back to their story: It's synchronistic that Vince Vaughn was a supporting actor in *Mr. and Mrs. Smith.* Vince and Jennifer began dating following Brad and Angelina's connection. This isn't the same type of Earth-moving experience as the Brangelina (dubbed by the media) relationship, but it's interesting to see where Jennifer rebounded during the chaos.

Here's Vince and Jennifer's BMP snapshot chart:

	VINCE VAUGHN	JENNIFER ANISTON
Birth date	March. 28, 1970	Feb. 11, 1969
Life Path #	12/3-Informed Communicator	20/2- Inward Creator
Astrology Sun	Aries-Charming	Aquarius- Out-of-the-Box
Major Sub-lesson #	1-Leader	11/2-Intuitive, In-the-moment
Minor Sub-lesson #	2-Inward Creator & 8-Physical Manifester	11, 1 & 1, Intuitive leader
Birth Order	First Born boy (two older sisters, unsure age difference, could make him Only)	First Born Girl (reports of three brothers)
Acceleration Points	3 & Aries mix results in high on charm, lower on detail. The 1 &2 sub-lessons are minor, but could create a leader who knows the value of listening and knows when to talk (may be a bit more of a talker, however). Being First Born boy with 1, 3, Aries and 8 creates an aggressive visionary with lots to say, and could challenge his listening skills.	2 accelerated with 0, 11/2, Aquarius shows very private, inward creator, and thinker. Can be fun and social but will be overloaded with too many people in a mix. She has superior listening, intuitive skills.

VINCE VAUGHN **BMP** SUMMARY:

Vince is one that prefers to lead through inspiration (Aries), usually with the spoken word (Life Path 3). With his 1 major influence, he is quite capable of pushing forward with a bit more force, and that Aries energy can turn into a very quick tongue when things are not going his way. His major sub-lesson is 2 (that of more of a listener and quiet creator), but most of his mix supports more extroverted behavior and actions. His mix would also point toward more of a visionary versus detailed person (1, 8, Aries, 3).

JENNIFER ANISTON & VINCE VAUGHN BMP SUMMARY:
The attraction to Jennifer Aniston is that she is a great supporter, listener, and has vision as a master number 11 (as previously mentioned). With 3, and Aries in Vince Vaughn's mix, Jennifer would be the calm to his storm. He has 2 as a sub-lesson in his mix so knows the value of inward processing, but has more of an extroverted mix (including his Life Path 1, and 8 sub-influences). On good days he would inspire, on bad days he may be a bit curt, and listening skills may shut down. Someone with an appreciation for a sensitive approach will find a good match with Jennifer's highly intuitive and creative mix.

Angelina, Brad, and others in the entertainment world are giving back to the world that has given them so much. It's fitting to spotlight those leaders that dedicate a great deal of time, sometimes their entire professional (and personal) lives, to making the world a better place.

Community Leaders

It takes commitment and sacrifice to champion causes. Those making ground-breaking commitments are rarely loved 100% by any one group. In fact, many times these people are hated, regardless of the goodness that results. The hatred and ugliness comes from jealousy, fear of change, judgment because old rules aren't being followed, and you can likely think of many more reasons. But it means taking a side, being open and passionate. There is no room for indifference with these couples. The passion that accompanies their work seems to cement their relationships as well. In writing about them, I salute them and their good work.

THE PEACEFUL WARRIORS—MARTIN LUTHER KING & CORETTA SCOTT KING

While most people are aware of these amazing figures, I'll give you a bit of the Kings' story.

Their story: Coretta was a singer by training (degree in voice and violin), and Martin a theologian, who became a pastor in the Baptist/Christian church. His work focuses on racial equality and his method is to achieve this through peaceful demonstration. I say this in the present as even after his death, his words have become truth for many today. Martin Luther King was shot and killed while doing his good work. But the story just begins there, as the day that King died, his wife Coretta Scott King picked up where he left off. The week following Reverend King's death, he was scheduled to attend another peaceful demonstration. Mrs. King attended in his absence. Over the years Mrs. King's support extended to women's rights, gay/lesbian rights, AIDS/HIV prevention and much more. And their commitment lives on as all four of the Kings' children went on to be active leaders in equality campaigns.

Here is the Kings' BMP snapshot chart:

	CORETTA SCOTT KING	MARTIN LUTHER KING
Birth date	April. 27, 1927	January 15, 1929
Life Path #	14/5-Unending Talent	10/1- Leader (accelerated)
Astrology Sun	Taurus-Stabilizer	Capricorn- Climber

Major Sub-lesson #	27/9-Humanitarian	15/6-Server, Responsible One
Minor Sub-lesson #	2-Inward Creator & 7-Source of Knowledge	1-Leader & 5-Unending Talent
Birth Order	Unknown (reports of younger brother, older sister)	Middle-Pleaser (second son of three boys)
Acceleration Points	This blend is an example of masculine and feminine balanced. 5 is best described as loud due to the constant activity and creation that goes on in a 5 world. This would be defined as more yang as a result. Then the 9 and 2 are about listening and people, so very ying. The 7, while an introverted number, can also be very firm in approach to beliefs so more yang. Taurus and 9 makes for a major people person. .	Capricorn, Life Path 1 (10/1 intensifies the leader with zero) accelerates a self-inflicted need to manifest success, and be an authority. The 1's and 5 in his mix would indicate that he was not a detailed person with a yang approach to most of BMP with exception to a Middle pleaser approach. With the 6 and Middle combination, it would be likely that we'd see service to others as a core value, with martyrdom (due to over-helping) a distinct possibility.

CORETTA SCOTT KING BMP SUMMARY:

A Life Path 5 thrives on new experiences, change, and freedom. Coretta Scott King was a change agent that had made, literally, a world of difference. The blessing that comes along with being a 5 is that Mrs. King would have been good at a lot of things. Her challenge would be to become great at a few things.

With her minor influence of 7, this would have given her the capacity to research a few things enough to truly become an expert. Her 9 humanitarian major influence would have likely made her an expert of people. The challenge with anyone having a 9 influence is that people drama clings like a magnet to these compassionate individuals. So, it becomes very important to create healthy boundaries.

Accelerators would be connected to the Taurus and 9 enjoying people in general (all people). Taurus has a talent for soothing situations. With this compassionate combination comes the problem of enabling others. The combination of Taurus with 5 creates struggles to focus and complete projects. The 5 is a "Jane of all trades" and that decreases focus on completion of any one project, or a project might be finished but the quality suffers.

MARTIN LUTHER KING BMP SUMMARY:

A Life Path 1 is the leader, and his is even more accelerated with the Life Path adding up to a 10 then 1. Then add the Capricorn to his mix and whamo, instant performance machine. There have been reports that when Martin Luther King was given an autopsy (upon his death), his heart/organs were up to ten years older than his physical body. His task was a great one and, in pushing so hard to succeed, his physical body was paying the price before he was fatally attacked. There are many sources that say stress is one of the top killers of Americans, and it manifests in many physical ways (heart attacks, breathing issues, asthma attacks, and the list goes on).

Other influences in Martin Luther's mix include the 6 responsible one/server, which is a number that is shared with the majority of the U.S. Presidents and First Ladies of the 20th and 21st centuries. This can also manifest into a hero mentality and over-helping. Of the U.S. Presidents having heart problems while in office, 6 was a prevalent number in their mixes. His Birth Order points to being a Middle child. If this is the case, then he would want to please and serve even more, and could border on being a martyr.

He also had 5 in his numbers as a minor influence. This made freedom, change, and new ideas very important ingredients in his lifetime. Most of Martin Luther King's mix would be more visionary than detailed.

CORETTA SCOTT KING & MARTIN LUTHER KING BMP SUMMARY:

As a Life Path 5 unending talent, Taurus stabilizer, with 9 humanitarian (major influence) 7 analytical (minor influence), Mrs. King could master multi-tasking as a mother and civil rights leader, stabilize chaotic situations and bring them down to earth, enjoy people and have the compassion for efforts focusing on life, liberty and the pursuit of happiness, and still have the analytical capability to bring credibility to a cause. While compassion was an influential part of her mix (9, Taurus), she had a more steadfast, analytical side as well.

Martin Luther King would have had a great deal of respect for his wife as she could easily zig as he zagged. He was helping to successfully define a new world, and do this through peaceful demonstration. With a Capricorn with a Life Path 1 influence, Martin Luther could have easily become frustrated and turned to a more forceful darker side, and likely had the power to even create a type of civil war. For instance, if he would have partnered with Malcolm "X," a Baptist/Christian converted Muslim who took a much more aggressive approach to the civil rights movement, we would have a much different outcome. But peaceful demonstration denotes compassion and, with Coretta's 9 influence, would have likely continued to give him strength to stay the course. His 6 server/responsible one was a great compliment to her 9 humanitarian as well. She understood his need to serve, and would have been committed to the cause that created a more perfect union as a 9.

They both had 5 influences in their birth mix. Freedom is one of the themes in this type of number, and they focused on this in a very big way.

From the equal rights cause, we spotlight those investing their self-made fortunes to narrow the differences between the rich and poor through technology education and more.

THE BUILDERS OF THE FUTURE
—BILL GATES & MELINDA GATES

Their story: Bill Gates was born to a comfortable family, and grew up in Seattle. By age 13 he was writing computer programs. While he was attending Harvard he started his own company, Microsoft. By his Junior year in college, he decided to leave Harvard and dedicate his time to his company. By the late 1990's and early 2000's, Gates wrote two *New York Times* Best Selling books and donated the proceeds to non-profits that support many causes, including supporting those in poverty, education, and healthcare. Known for his philanthropy as well, he has donated billions of dollars to sharing technology education with the less fortunate. Today Gates is one of the richest people in the world. Melinda met Bill when working for Microsoft, and they were married in the early 1990's. She earned degrees in computer science and economics from Duke University and also earned her MBA. In the early 2000's, Melinda and Bill both decided to re-align their professional commitments to managing their charitable organization, Melinda and Bill Gates Foundation.

Here is the Gates' BMP snapshot chart:

	MELINDA GATES	BILL GATES
Birth date	August 15, 1964	October 28, 1955
Life Path #	16/7-Source of Knowledge	4-Builder of Order

Astrology Sun	Leo-Leader of the Pride	Scorpio-Patient Achiever
Major Sub-lesson #	15/6-Server	28/1-Leader
Minor Sub-lesson #	1-Leader & 5-Unending Talent	2-Inward Creator & 8-Physical Manifester
Birth Order	Unknown	First Born Boy (older, and younger sister)
Acceleration Points	Leo and 6 would result in a generosity streak, and need to oversee a community. The 7 is the analytical Melinda and creates a need for a certain amount of alone-time (if she were, for instance, an Only child this would accelerate her need for this as well).	As a 4 builder of order Bill wrote computer languages to run computer systems, the ultimate method man. The 2, and Scorpio would increase his preference to create alone. The Scorpio (strategic thinker) and 4 would increase his likelihood of having a clear vision as to direction of a project, or life in general. Some might call this stubborn.

MELINDA GATES BMP SUMMARY:

Put a Leo and 6 together and it's a good thing that the Gates have a large bank account. The biggest lesson when these two traits come together is to have bank accounts match the generosity of this mix. Melinda is really living her dream as she is able to impact the world at large (her Leo and 6 community) by funding so many causes through her (and her husband's) foundation. The 5 in her prefers freedom to do many things which can lead to focus issues because she would be good at a lot of things. Her Life Path 7 does add a balancing effect. With 7 energy, she would research a bit more (becoming the expert 7), judge a bit more harshly, and listen a bit more intently.

Bill Gates BMP Summary Mix:

Like he laid foundation for the computer world with Microsoft, he continues his good work as a philanthropist. As a Life Path 4, Gates would be more of a hands-on, method man. What may cause him stress is when others go outside of the foundation that he put in place. As First Born boy, and Life Path 1, this accelerates the 4 need to put processes in place as a control device. With the success he has demonstrated over the years, those that have followed his direction have prospered.

And speaking of prospering, Bill has a minor influence of 8. He is the poster child of being a physical manifester. His Scorpio tendencies as one with internal passion, but not one that outwardly expresses this, have not been as big an issue in his early days because his job was to sit, think and create on his own. With this mix, particularly as a younger man, Bill would have been more of a creative loner with a very small group of inner circle friends.

Melinda & Bill Gates BMP Summary:

Melinda would understand Bill's need to inwardly (Scorpio) visualize, create and be the #1 lead as her mix includes Leo leader, and 7 (loner) expert researcher. The 6 in Melinda is organized with the objective of serving others. The 4 in Bill invents in a similar way, but to create a well-oiled machine (in essence). Hers is a more people-oriented mix. So while they are both born to lead, they lead differently. While they both create foundation, they create this differently.

Melinda would be able to get Bill to open up a bit more being a charming Leo, and political 6 (meaning she wants to please and to serve people and organizations she cares about). Her mix is a bit more extroverted, while his is a bit more introverted. As long as she has artful ways to get Bill to communicate, then their relationship will remain strong. Being forceful with a Life Path 1, Scorpio, with 8 influences can lead to frustration, and deep-seated resentment on his part. It's helpful if Melinda recognizes, and deals functionally with, passive-aggressive behavior that may be a part of her husband's mix because Scorpio's rarely forget.

Moving to another self-made philanthropist.

RAGS TO RICHES
(WHAT DOESN'T KILL YOU MAKES YOU STRONGER)
—OPRAH & STEDMAN

I put Oprah in the community leaders section because of her many charitable projects. From opening schools in South Africa, to her involvement in many U.S. causes, she is truly committed to the betterment of others. Without her physical presence, the world would not be as great a place to live in. Am I exaggerating? I just did an AOL poll and it asked, "Who do you respect the most in the world?" It included people like Margaret Thatcher—former UK Prime Minister, Nancy Pelosi—the first U.S. woman speaker of the House, Hillary Clinton, and the like. And Oprah Winfrey was listed. Who do you think made the number one slot? Starts with an "O" and ends with an "h."

Her story (oh, and Stedman): No disrespect to Mr. Graham, as he is obviously doing well for himself. He grew up in a functional setting, received his undergraduate and masters degrees, and became an entrepreneur. Oprah is a bit more transparent given her history—magically self-made, healed, bright, kind, compassionate, and generous. Born to unwed, poor parents, nothing was in her favor. She grew into a troubled youth, began experimenting with drugs in her early teens, was sexually molested, and was pregnant at the age of 14. Following the premature birth and death of her baby, she turned her life around and moved to Nashville to live with her father. Reports say that he was more disciplined and stable, and this allowed her to excel in school, and in life. When she was 19 she worked in a radio station, tried college for a while but dropped out to become an anchor on one of the local television stations (the first black woman to hold that position). Opportunities led her to Chicago where she developed the show Oprah. Dubbed the Queen of the Daytime Talk Shows, she also is the third woman in the American entertainment world to own her own studio (Lucille Ball was one of the first as well), is also a gifted actor, and has produced a number of movies. Today she is the most powerful and influential woman in television, according to *Forbes* magazine, but 200,000+ AOL survey respondents (in 2006) would say she's even bigger than many elected world leaders!

And what of Stedman? There have been rumors for years that Oprah and Stedman were planning to marry, but details really aren't known to the public. While inquiring minds want to know everything about Oprah, it's great that she has some privacy. They have been companions for some time, so let's take a closer snapshot at why they mix so well.

	OPRAH WINFREY	STEDMAN GRAHAM
Birth date	January 29, 1954	March 6, 1951
Life Path #	13/4-Builder of Order	16/7-Source of Knowledge
Astrology Sun	Aquarius-Out-of-the-Box	Pisces-Intuitive
Major Sub-lesson #	11/2-Intuitive	6-Server
Minor Sub-lesson #	11-Intuitive & 1 &1 Double Leader	6-Server
Birth Order	Only	Unknown

| Acceleration Points | Innovating intuitively is accelerated by the Aquarian, and 11. Detachment from people is accelerated with Only, Aquarian, 11. | Creating truth and to be considered truthful is doubly important to a mix with 7 and 6. Reliability is a trait 7 and 6 can share, while expressed in different ways (7 thru accurate analysis, 6 thru need to honestly serve others). |

OPRAH WINFREY **BMP** SUMMARY:

At a young age, Oprah learned that order was the way to turn herself around. As an Only child she had a knack (when she finally chose to set goals) for setting goals and reaching them. Embracing her Life Path 4 as a builder of process, order, foundation, to overcome her life challenges, resulted in a rags to riches story. One of the keys to success with this Life Path is perseverance. Some of the challenges that come along with this path are persevering to the point of overworking and not keeping an eye on her health, being too reliable as a friend, life partner, and professional. The 4 can judge harshly when something doesn't fit into her box, but the Aquarian in her was able to create boxes with flexibility. She was able to create a foundation around creativity, change, and differing ideas. The 11 is a major influence to her leadership ability (being first in so many arenas), and moving forward on faith, and trusting her intuition. This is a number to maximize in-the-moment experiences, the Aquarian also moves in this direction as an out-of-the-box social butterfly. Dysfunctional behavior would be over partaking, overeating, doing drugs, drinking alcohol and perceiving this to be fun. Functionally would be, well, what we see

Oprah doing today. However, the Aquarian, 11, with the Only child influence would need to take a break from people. She was trained as an Only to process on her own. She has to re-energize, and cleanse (other people's stuff) inwardly because she takes on a lot of energy psychically (11). Aquarians need time to quietly create at times. On the Aquarian note, Oprah is the poster child for Aquarians—she is very generous (2006 she took 1000+ people—employees and their families to Hawaii, threw Legend's Ball to honor accomplished black women and gave them diamonds!...), likable, enjoys working on the cutting edge, out-of-the-box. All in all it's a balanced feminine/ying (Aquarian, 11), masculine/yang (4, Only) mix.

STEDMAN GRAHAM **BMP** SUMMARY:

Stedman's mix is slightly more of a ying mix with the Pisces intuitive (ying), 7 analyzer (while can be quiet, can be a yang approach), with a 6 server, responsible one that can be more of a cosmic father that likes to help others move forward/heal (ying). Being an overseer of a chosen community as a 6, being perceived as being truthful is important—"trust me I'm your father" kind of thing. The 7 analyzes certain subjects (not all) to create truth—"I've researched, and understand this" and that makes it truth. The 6 can be very charismatic, while the 7 can be quietly and knowledgeably convincing. The 6 tends to be personally reliable, the 7 is reliable in his chosen areas of study/analysis. The intuitive Pisces is faith based (trust in yourself, and your impressions of others) while the 7 is about trusting in the research, and not trusting others. If people disappointed Stedman in the past then this could create a man that is suspicious about truth, and lacks faith (in himself as well as others). If he has trusted his intuition, been truthful and reliable, he will attract those types of people and situations into his life.

OPRAH & STEDMAN **BMP** SUMMARY:

Oprah and Stedman have a number of things in common in their birth mixes, but express them in different ways. Intuitively, Oprah is an 11, Stedman is Pisces. Socially, Stedman is a charismatic, cosmic father 6. Oprah is a social, generous Aquarian. Oprah is a 4 builder of foundation. Stedman builds through 7 research and 6 organizational skills. If functionally developed, they both have an appreciation for a grounded approach to certain situations, while having faith in their inner voices as well. You might hear either one of them say, "something tells me to..." and they will do their best work, partnering, relationships, listening to this without question.

From self-made to royal heirs, their lives can be as dramatic as Hollywood, but integral to making the world a better place.

THE ROYALS—PRINCESS DIANA, PRINCE CHARLES, DODI FAYED, & PRINCESS CAMILLA

I'll say up-front that I don't understand royalty titles. I am certain that someone who knows how aristocratic and royalty titles work will say, "Michelle, you are supposed to address them as..." So let's move on. I put the Royal family under community because they not only define their country, England, but Lady Diana represented compassion and kindness to the world.

Their story: Diana married Charles in the summer of 1981. I was to enter college that next month. Everything came to a stand-still to watch the royal wedding, some reports saying that nearly 750,000 million people watched the royal wedding on that day. Married at only 20 years old, Diana was of aristocratic and royal heritage, and thirteen years Charles' junior, the perfect "political" fit for the heir to the throne of England. Diana "delivered" two male heirs to the throne, and kept her title as a member of the royal family after their divorce fifteen years later. She became well-known, respected and loved for her philanthropy work during her short life.

Here is Charles & Diana's BMP snapshot chart:

	PRINCESS DIANA	PRINCE CHARLES
Birth date	July 1, 1961	November 14, 1948
Life Path #	16/7-Source of Knowledge	38/11-Intuitive
Astrology Sun	Cancer-Comforter	Scorpio-Patient Achiever
Major Sub-lesson #	1-Leader	14/5-Unending Talent
Minor Sub-lesson #	1-Leader	1-Leader &4- Builder of Order
Birth Order	Youngest Girl (two older sisters, one younger brother)	First Born Boy
Acceleration Points	Diana's Cancer and 7 mix would likely keep her from sharing feelings to protect herself from being hurt or threatening her definition of truth. This would keep her from expressing her major emphasis as a 1 leader as well, if not overcome.	As an 11, Charles would be very perceptive and inward focused. This inward focus is increased with the Scorpio Sun Sign.

PRINCESS DIANA **BMP SUMMARY:**

Diana became known for her passion to help others in less fortunate situations. The 7 in her is that seeker of truth, and the Cancer is the cosmic mother. The 7 is more of an inward processing individual. The Cancer, while loving others, and loving to be loved by others, puts up a shield of protection to keep from being hurt emotionally. So that she could come out of her shell and truly make an impact, there was a point in her life where she sought professional mentoring to better her public communication abilities. In a passive way, she was able to express her leadership in the royal family "delivering" two males as heirs to the throne which earned her a position in the royal family, even after divorce. Once embracing her professional training, she could truly express her major sub-influence as a 1 world leader, and communicate her compassionate truth.

Prince Charles BMP Summary:

As an 11 intuitive, Charles would be able to read people and situations very well. But an 11 is an inward processing number and, add Scorpio to the mix with immense inward passion, the result is a man of few words. His major sub-influence is a 5 unending talent which would say that Charles is likely to be good at many things, and has to be going somewhere or doing something all the time. The 4 minor sub-influence would point to him being a hands-on doer. This could point to the possibility that Charles must be able to experience and handle things for himself before he takes anything on as his truth.

Princess Diana & Prince Charles BMP Summary:

When you have two people who have a tendency not to openly communicate then you have the potential makings of disaster. Diana would be more of an analyzer to get to a truth. Charles is more intuitive as an 11 with the 5 capability of taking on projects quickly, gathering details on his Scorpio terms. Analyzer versus intuitive can work in a relationship as long as an appreciation for these differences is established. Unfortunately, we know that this was an unsuccessful partnership.

BACK TO THE STORY: Rumors, scandals, separation and finally divorce, photos emerged with Dodi Fayed and Diana on holiday and traveling. Dodi was the son of an Egyptian billionaire, and his mother was sister to a famous arms dealer. His profession, however, was regularly referred to as "film producer." They met their unfortunate deaths together in Paris in a car accident.

	PRINCESS DIANA	DODI FAYED
Birth date	July 1, 1961	April 15, 1955
Life Path #	16/7-Source of Knowledge	12/3-Informed Communicator
Astrology Sun	Cancer-Comforter	Taurus-Stabilizer
Major Sub-lesson #	1-Leader	15/6-Server
Minor Sub-lesson #	1-Leader	1-Leader &5-Unending Talent
Birth Order	Youngest Girl (two older sisters, one younger brother)	First Born Boy
Acceleration Points	Diana's Cancer and 7 mix would likely keep her from sharing feelings to protect herself from being hurt, or threatening her definition of truth. This would keep her from expressing her major emphasis as a 1 leader as well, if not overcome.	With major # 6 server and Taurus stabilizer this makes Dodi a people person, and he would highly respect Diana's philanthropy efforts as a result. This mix of 3, 6, 1, 5 would say that he would prefer not to handle small details.

DODI FAYED BMP SUMMARY:

Dodi has a very social mix with Life Path 3, Taurus, 6, 1, and 5 in his Birth Mix. This mix was also more likely to communicate outwardly (versus Charles' inward tendencies). In any relationship, if someone doesn't bring issues out in the open, then they will likely never be resolved. With a 6 and Taurus, this would likely accelerate his hope for a better world, which would include reaching out to people. While Dodi's family was very wealthy, his chosen trade was film production and he worked on a number of great projects. Having a Life Path 3, this was the ultimate way to communicate internationally and be heard. Having the 5 influence of unending talent, this would also fulfill his need for regular change, new ideas, and new experiences. This mix would also indicate that Dodi did not prefer to be involved in the small details. However with a 6 major influence, he could get involved enough to set up processes for others to follow, and then step out for other people to execute.

PRINCESS DIANA & DODI FAYED BMP SUMMARY:
Diana being 7, and Cancer, as discussed earlier in this section makes for a more private person. Dodi was anything but shy. As a Life Path 3 he is one that enjoys communicating outwardly, and Diana could fill in certain blanks with details as a 7. Dodi had a major influence of 6, and a Taurus Sun Sign which loves people, supports causes to help others, and make the world a better place. Of course, Diana was one of the cosmic mothers of her time, and with that her chosen love interest would have to have a big appreciation for her work. Diana would have found Dodi's background in movies and working with actors to be eye opening, as well as his 3 tendencies, as he could serve as a bit of a coach for her when public speaking. There were many win:win's in this relationship.

BACK TO THE STORY: Charles had a love in his life pre-dating his relationship with Diana. It was Camilla. During Charles and Diana's fifteen years of marriage (through the 80's and into the mid-90's), Charles was photographed many times with Camilla on holiday. No one knows the full story except the participants, but after Diana's tragic death, Charles and Camilla were wed.

The BMP snapshot chart of Camilla and Charles looks like this:

	PRINCESS CAMILLA	PRINCE CHARLES
Birth date	July 17, 1947	November 14, 1948
Life Path #	18/9-Humanitarian	38/11-Intuitive
Astrology Sun	Cancer-Comforter	Scorpio-Patient Achiever
Major Sub-lesson #	8-Physical Manifester	14/5-Unending Talent
Minor Sub-lesson #	1-Leader & 7 Source of Knowledge	1-Leader &4- Builder of Order
Birth Order	First Born Girl (one younger sister, one younger brother)	First Born Boy
Acceleration Points	Camilla's Cancer and 9 mix would likely create someone that has a great love for comforting others and causes, but would also be caught up in a great deal of people dramas. This mix would have difficulty letting go of relationships (even cling). The 8 manifester and Cancer mix may have a tendency to hoard certain things in the physical.	As an 11, Charles would be very perceptive, and inward focused. This inward focus is increased with the Scorpio Sun Sign.

PRINCESS CAMILLA'S BMP SUMMARY:

What's interesting about Camilla's mix is it is very similar to Princess Diana's. Camilla's Life Path 9, and Cancer Sun Sign would accelerate her interest in people and their well-being. This would also accelerate issues of letting go of people and their dramas. With this mix, it takes time, and strong boundaries to end relationships that continue to be unhealthy (this mix would make many excuses for the negative situations). The Cancer and 8 mix would point to the possibility of hoarding certain things in the physical (sometimes a protection mechanism). She does have some influences in her mix to help her create boundaries. The 8 physical manifester, and being First Born would create strength to pull away from certain situations, especially if it threatened physical acquirements. She has a 7 detail/analyzer sub-lesson number like Diana, but Camilla's mix has a bit more outward communication ability and lower in need for detail (8, and First Born is more outward, and yang).

Princess Camilla & Prince Charles BMP Summary:
Camilla's Life Path 9 and Cancer Sun Sign would accelerate her interest in people and their well-being. This would also accelerate issues of letting go of people and their dramas. If Charles didn't officially end his relationship directly with Camilla, being more inward processing and a mix that exchanges fewer words (11 and Scorpio particularly), he could have come in and out of Camilla's life if she didn't set boundaries. The 8 physical manifester, and being First Born is more yang and outward and would help Camilla more aggressively draw communication out of Charles.

Within the same year, and venue, of Camilla and Prince Charles ceremony, was an even more popular couple. It was royalty in a bit more liberal circle.

Same Gender Partnerships:

This is a very important section in this book to demonstrate that masculine or yang doesn't only mean male, and feminine or ying doesn't only mean female. It also shows that love is expressed in many ways. Some would call this "Same Sex Marriage" ("same gender" is actually a more accurate description), but upon writing this book, gay couples have been forbidden in the majority of the U.S. and the world to marry legally. What no one can argue is that the more love is freely expressed in the world, the healthier it is.

ROCKET MEN—ELTON JOHN & DAVID FURNISH

Their story: Elton John and David Furnish are among the first famous same gender couples to enter into a civil partnership in England. They had been in a committed relationship for eleven years prior to their commitment to one another. Their ceremony was performed in the same venue, the Guildhall, as Prince Charles and Camilla Parker Bowles in the same year (2006). I've made an assumption that everyone knows who Elton John is. A pop star since the 1970's, he's crafted music from a variety of genres, and charted a Top 40 single every year from 1970 through 1996. Many of his songs are staples in the music world including: *Rocket Man*, *Goodbye Yellow Brick Road*, and *Don't Let The Sun Go Down On Me*. His dynamic, flamboyant, charismatic (not to mention great voice), style is one likely to never be topped. David is a film-maker, producer and director.

Here is the BMP snapshot of Elton and David's chart:

	ELTON JOHN	DAVID FURNISH
Birth date	March. 25, 1947	October 25, 1962
Life Path #	13/4-Builder of Order	17/8-Physical Manifester
Astrology Sun	Aries-Charming Leader	Scorpio-Patient Achiever
Major Sub-lesson #	25/7-Analyzer, Source of Knowledge	25/7-Analyzer, Source of Knowledge

Minor Sub-lesson #	2-Inward Creator & 5-Unending Talent	2-Inward Creator & 5-Unending Talent
Birth Order	Unknown	Unknown (older, and younger brother)
Acceleration Points	The Life Path 4, and 7 major sub-lesson would create a more detailed foundation builder. This mix is very diverse as Builder, inspirer, analyzer, and multi-tasker. Very active.	The Scorpio, 7 is an indication that this is a bit more of an inward mix—detailed, and strategic. The 2 wouldn't be as significant if not for the above-mentioned.

ELTON JOHN BMP SUMMARY:

Elton has an eclectic mix. His Aries moves him to inspire—his stage presence is unforgettable. The 4 is one that builds great things from scratch—being a pop idol with singles in the Top 40 for nearly 30 years for example. The 7 influence gives him a knack, and detail-ability, for being a specialist in his chosen field. The 5 (while minor) creates an interest in variety—similar to what is demonstrated through his music. He's an inspiring, detailed thinking builder. His 4 and 7 can take him aggressively inward which would be perceived as more of a yang/masculine quality. Once his "truth" and process have been established, he may become stubborn and opinionated. Because the activity is so high with this mix—thinking, building, doing, Aries vocalizing—this would be more of a yang personality.

DAVID FURNISH BMP SUMMARY:

David has more of an inward quality about him with his Scorpio patience, and 7 loner/analyzer traits. As a Life Path 8, this gives him the cosmic ability to generate wealth in the physical or lose it as easily. Why?

Because physical manifestation flows for this Life Path, and taken for granted it will always be there, then an accumulation strategy (saving, investing) is never adopted. However, with the Scorpio, 7 influence things get a bit more detailed, more planned, and hence more stabilized money (or whatever physical things are important to David). A word on spirituality with this mix, he would be very literal, and likely have challenges taking leaps of faith. This mix would also be more yang in nature, but expressed more inwardly.

Elton John & David Furnish BMP Summary:

Does it mean that when you have two primarily yang/masculine people in relationship that it won't work? Elton and David share the same day of birth so they both have an appreciation for someone needing to analyze (7), and like to be busy (5) with a variety of activities. David would tend to be more of the Scorpio introvert in the relationship, while Elton would be the Aries extrovert. David would be more of the visionary manager (8), with Elton being the builder of the process being managed. It's a very nice fit, as they have enough in common (2, 5, 7), and enough complementary points (Aries, Scorpio, 8, 4) to have a solid relationship. For clarity, any couple with complementary mixes can also be interpreted as opposites. If opposites have an appreciation for qualities that they don't have, then relationships work. Elton and David have had more than a decade to know that they are in love and committed to one another.

As a Birth Mix Patterns Master, I don't buy into the concept that we can't relate to with one another. Life is full of choices. If we make the choice to understand ourselves, then we can also understand why we react to certain personalities the way we do. For example, let's say you are buying a car, and you aren't quite as detailed, which also might mean you aren't as patient. What if your life partner, husband, wife has a knack for looking at miles per gallon, performance, safety rankings, and the like. Doesn't that make your (less detailed personality) purchase that much better? Someone who doesn't appreciate the full gamut of personality differences might decide to put a person down because he/she isn't thinking just like him/her. Think before you judge. That person unlike you may strengthen your weaknesses.

Now we go from music to dancing.

DANCIN' QUEENS
—ELLEN DEGENERES & PORTIA DE ROSSI

Their story: Ellen DeGeneres has been known as a popular talk show host in the 2000's, with one of her trademarks being casual, pop music dancing. Prior to this (among other things), she built her career as a stand-up comic, and her television shows (including *Ellen*). Early in her career she'd been honored/recognized by Johnny Carson, Showtime, and received Emmy's. A major turning point for Ellen was in 1997 when she made a controversial announcement. She is twelve years older than I am, and I remember the media frenzy. Ellen made history for two reasons: Her character in her television series announced that she was gay, and two weeks prior to her television character announcing this, Ellen announced that she was gay. Following both announcements, her television series began to focus on life as a gay woman and was cancelled the next season (some say it was due to low ratings, and others say it was the content). While not really looking to make political statements, she has become another mapmaker to bring diverse lifestyles out into the open.

Portia is a very sexy woman. While she has had a lengthy career, she became known for her role on the popular television series *Ally McBeal* in the 1990's. Her physical look is very feminine, with beautiful long blonde hair. While she breaks the mold on stereotyping that if you are a lesbian you look like a man, she has voiced frustration. She reported in an *Advocate* interview that when she finally announced that she was gay, people wouldn't believe her.

Here is the BMP snapshot chart of Ellen and Portia:

	ELLEN DeGENERES	PORTIA DE ROSSI
Birth date	January. 26, 1958	January 31, 1973
Life Path #	14/5-Unending Talent	7-Source of Knowledge
Astrology Sun	Aquarius-Out of the Box	Aquarius-Out of the Box
Major Sub-lesson #	26/8-Physical Manifester	31/4-Builder of Process
Minor Sub-lesson #	2-Inward Creator & 6-Server	3-Expert Communicator & 1-Leader
Birth Order	First Born Girl (one brother four years age difference)	Unknown
Acceleration Points	The Life Path 5, and Aquarian Sun would point to a mix that could lack focus—5 need for variety and bored easily, and Aquarian dreamy yet social. These two traits also accelerate creative idea generating.	The Aquarian, 7 is an indication that Portia may need distance from others at times (perceived as having an emotional shell around her). It may look like she lacks passion, but it's really because she is in her own inward world. Add 4 and she is busy getting things in order.

ELLEN DEGENERES **BMP** SUMMARY:

Ellen is a balanced ying/feminine (Aquarius, 2, 6), and yang/masculine (5, 8) mix. The Aquarian has an intuitive sense of what would work in the future. This results in an out-of-the-box creator. With these ideas comes a very busy mind. Combining with the 5 energy, ideas multiply quickly, it becomes important that someone with this mix come up with a process to focus on fully executing ideas. A challenge that a 5 might have is to also complete projects with good quality. Sometimes 5's get task-oriented and squeak by on quality for the sake of calling something finished. The Sun Sign and numbers would say that this is a person that is more of a visionary, and less detailed.

PORTIA DE ROSSI **BMP** SUMMARY:

Portia is a bit more inward in her birth mix. While an Aquarian can be social, she also has many images playing in her mind that can distract her from outward activities. This is accelerated by her 7 analyzing approach which is more inward and more detailed. A major influencing number is also 4, and is one that creates foundation and method. So Portia has two thinker numbers, and an idea generating Sun Sign (if she were an Only child this would accelerate internalizing as well). That's a lot of internal dialogue. As minor influences she does have 3 that helps her find her voice (can be through many channels of communication), and her Aquarian Sun also helps her turn on the people-love-me charm. Many may perceive Portia as very ying/feminine in personality due to her internal focus, but the noise in this type of mixes' head can get quite aggressive. In addition, she has the potential to become stubborn (Aquarian, 4, 7) once the out-of–the-box ideas have been researched, declared her truth, and become implanted into a process. It's a lot of work to rewire this detailed process.

Ellen DeGeneres & Portia de Rossi BMP Summary:

Ellen and Portia met in the early 2000's in a professional setting. Portia said in an interview with the *Advocate* that Ellen took her breath away when they met. Both Aquarians, they may have had a future view of the great quality of life they would have together. While they have the same Sun Sign, the rest of their mix is quite different. Ellen's mix supports a personality that is more of a visionary. Portia's mix supports a personality that gets into the details, and builds foundation. As a team, Ellen can generate many ideas/visions, and if she has the patience and interest in quality, Portia can research and create process around them.

And now moving from more subtle gay rights activists to a triangle that lives and speaks loudly on the subject.

And Twins Make 4
—Melissa Etheridge, Tammy Lynn Michaels
& Julie Cypher

Their story: Melissa Etheridge is an accomplished rock 'n' roll singer and has won two (to date) Grammy awards for Best Female Rock Vocal Performance. In the early 2000's she was diagnosed with breast cancer, and as a talented artist brought more attention to the breast cancer cause by writing and performing *I Run for Life.* She has been a gay rights activist, publicly announcing this in 1993 during Bill Clinton's first inauguration.

Etheridge has two children with Julie Cypher (they met while Julie was directing her music video). The sperm donor for both children was guitarist, singer, and songwriter David Crosby. Cypher returned to a heterosexual lifestyle and married (a man) in 2004.

Tammy Lynn Michaels Etheridge and Melissa Etheridge were

married in September 2003. Tammy gave birth to twins in the Fall of 2006 (sperm from an anonymous donor). Tammy is an actress, primarily in television.

Here is the Melissa's and Julie's snapshot chart:

	MELISSA ETHERIDGE	JULIE CYPHER
Birth date	May. 29, 1961	August 24, 1964
Life Path #	24/6-Server	7-Source of Knowledge
Astrology Sun	Gemini- Change Agent	Virgo-Detailed Expander
Astrology Sun	29/11-Intuitive	24/6-Server
Major Sub-lesson #	2-Inward Creator & 9-Humanitarian	2-Inward Creator & 4-Process Builder
Minor Sub-lesson #	Unknown	Unknown
Acceleration Points	The Life Path 6, and 9 supports being an activist to create a better world, and serve others.	The Virgo, 7 indicates a very detailed person.

MELISSA ETHERIDGE BMP SUMMARY:

Melissa has Life Path 6 server, with 9 humanitarian influences as well. This indicates that she would be one that wants to serve a community, and to make it a better place. It also shows that she would be a people person. The downside is she could be an enabler (over-helper of others), and needlessly get caught up in people's dramas. This could end with people taking advantage of her financially and in other ways. When she is in a balanced place mentally, and physically, she could listen more closely to her 11 influence as an intuitive to back away from situations that don't serve her. The key is to listen and trust her gut reaction.

What makes her an awesome spokesperson (in addition to the above qualities) for gay rights, breast cancer, or any other cause is her suave Gemini communication skills. This Sun Sign embraces change, new ideas, and products. If the causes, products, ideas, don't keep her interested, however, the personality tendency is to be a bit fickle.

Julie Cypher BMP Summary:

Julie is doubly likely to be detailed with Virgo and 7 in her mix. A person with this mix is hungry to know the facts, and will communicate in a very accurate way. For instance, a bank balance might be $1,231.16 as opposed to a little over $1200. The server 6 has a major influence on this mix as well. The community that this mix would serve would be able to rely on Julie for finite answers, and could hand her any project and it would be 7 analyzed, Virgo improved, 4 (minor #) organized, 6 targeted to a community that will be aided/healed. It's very Virgo, 7 that the sperm donor to Melissa and Julie's two children was specifically announced, both children were from the same donor, he was researched and very intentionally chosen for his musical talent (to accurately match Melissa's talent).

Melissa Etheridge & Julie Cypher BMP Summary:

Melissa and Julie have a similar draw to serve community with the 6 server/ responsible one influence. They both are activists in the gay rights arena, but get there a little differently. Melissa had a softer, ying, approach as a humanitarian, while Julie's Virgo serves the greater good through detailed order approach (more yang). The Gemini in Melissa likes change and will do that on more of an intuitive (11) level, while Julie would be more cautious and research possibilities before moving forward. Their children have a very well-rounded demonstration of research, versus intuitive approaches.

BACK TO THEIR STORY: In approximately 2000 Julie and Melissa split because Julie was reconsidering her sexuality. There are reports that Melissa and Tammy met that following year. They were married in 2003, and had twins in 2006. So what makes them such a great match?

The Etheridges' BMP snapshot chart is as follows:

	MELISSA ETHERIDGE	TAMMY ETHERIDGE
Birth date	May. 29, 1961	November 26, 1974
Life Path #	24/6-Server	22 (4)-Material & Humanitarian Master
Astrology Sun	Gemini- Change Agent	Sagittarius-Life Partaker
Major Sub-lesson #	29/11 (2)-Intuitive	26/8-Physical Manifester
Minor Sub-lesson #	2-Inward Creator & 9-Humanitarian	2-Inward Creator & 6-Server
Birth Order	Unknown	Unknown
Acceleration Points	The Life Path 6, and 9 supports being an activist to create a better world, and serve others.	The 22 is a master number—the 4 is parenthesis to show that 22 can be reduced to a lower number depending on choices made—and accelerates the 8 manifester potential, and 6 server potential.

TAMMY ETHERIDGE **BMP** SUMMARY:

Tammy has a master number of 22. This means that Tammy has the potential to master monetary and spiritual/humanitarian efforts in this lifetime. If she decided not to do this, her number would be reduced to a 4 (2+2). This is neither good nor bad, it just comes down to choices in this lifetime. Some attendees to my workshops have been uncomfortable with the idea that we have free will (in my opinion) in the matter of our birth mixes. But if we didn't have some choices then all that our lives would mean is that we have failed. I can't believe that the Universe would be so cruel. But back to Tammy. Obviously, being so high profile, she has chosen 22. This accelerates her likelihood of achieving great things in the physical including money (8), and serving humanity (6). Not quite as detailed, and research-oriented, the sperm donor to Melissa and Tammy's twins was anonymous.

Melissa & Tammy Etheridge BMP Summary:

Melissa and Tammy have an accelerated interest as partners in serving community (6, 22), and humanitarian efforts (9, 22) . They both are activists in the gay rights arena, got married, Tammy took Melissa's name, and they now have twins. It is a life statement. The Gemini in Melissa likes change and will do that on more of an intuitive (11 master number) level. Tammy, as a Sagittarius, enjoys freedom, is the life of a party, is a great networker, and looks for ways to unite people to make a better world. This combination equals partners that have a great time together, have potential to make a major impact on the gay rights movement and other causes they sponsor like breast cancer research. They would likely need to hire a detailed assistant as their combined mixes support more vision than nuts and bolts.

III. How the Elements Expand BMP Communication

Water, Wood, Fire, Metal, Earth

In each of the *Birth Mix Patterns* series (this is the third), I have introduced additional elements into the process to further understand ourselves and others. This book is no exception. In the 1990's I was trained professionally in feng shui (by Penny Crabtree, author of *Feng Shui Dynamics*). When doing Birth Mix Patterns, and even hypnotherapy and NLP (Neuro-Linguistic Programming™) sessions, external elements regularly come to mind to help my clients balance the ying and yang in their environments. The concept that occurred to me is if one was feeling, say, unsupported in connection with work then elements were also missing. Maybe her Birth Mix was Virgo, Life Path 8, with major influences of 1, and 7, First Born—very accurate, detailed, manager. Let's say she is an executive with a beautiful wood desk and matching furniture in earth tones, nice (live and healthy) plants, a soothing water element by her door (in her career area), her walls are a neutral green, she has some great windows that look out onto a city landmark, but she feels sluggish, and unmotivated to crunch the numbers that she could when she was a junior employee. Guess what's missing for an accurate manager like this? Metal and fire are missing. But most important is the metal as this is an element of accuracy, one that feeds her biggest personal asset to moving up the corporate ladder as a detailed Virgo, with 7 influences.

Let's say as this same professional was moving up the ranks, she had the utilitarian metal desk, metal cabinets, white walls, grey carpet, and she brought in a water element for her career area, had some live healthy plants, and a window (not the greatest view, but it's a window). She found that she was being too detailed all the time. Her managers were asking her to get to the point when they'd stop by her office for an explanation on something. The more she ran numbers, the more numbers she felt she had to look at. She felt overwhelmed. Why? Too much metal that accelerated her tendency to be very detailed.

Of course, you always want to balance the elements in your home and office. While the following shows some similarities to feng shui, this is more about the emotional and physical support that these elements stir and how they accelerate, decelerate and neutralize Birth Mix Patterns. The elements I'll focus on in relation to BMP are water, wood, fire, metal, and earth.

ELEMENT	GOALS SUPPORTED	ITEMS	COLORS	SHAPES
Water	Activating career, encouraging new projects, seeking activity, change (you never step in the same stream twice)	Fountains, anything with glass, mirrors, fish tanks (rapid and rippling water create different energy)	Black, reflective dark blue	Waves, "S" curves

Element	Goals Supported	Items	Colors	Shapes
Wood	General health, and healthy living, love of family, seeking comfort, consistent loving relationships (family, siblings, children, spouse)	Anything wood	Greens, blues (not reflective)	Columns (like a tree standing up)
Metal	Seeking accuracy/precision, interest in detail, and/ or research	All metals	White, very light pastels, metallic colors	Round, dome-like
Earth	Seeking balance, being grounded, putting down your roots, seeking support from your environment	Soil, clay, terra cotta, large stones, heavy pottery, and sculpture stabilize	Earth tones, brown, earthy yellows and brown/oranges	Square
Fire	Seeking passion, heating up a situation, getting noticed, lighting a fire under/ activating good relationships	Anything associated with fire, leather, things with electrical charge (includes pictures of people), animals	Red	Pyramid shapes, Pointing up

In Native American tradition, and others, they also honor air (as does Astrology). For this exercise, the presumption is air is contained in all the mentioned elements—air feeds fire, carbon dioxide/oxygen exchanges with plants, air joins with water (air bubbles, fish exchanging carbon dioxide/oxygen). If air is an integral element to your practice however, please add your own notes to the chart.

Here's a story to demonstrate the elements in connection with Birth Mix Patterns. My friend had just gotten married and merged households.

They were both in their thirties so they had an ample amount of time to create living environments that supported each of them. She was much more ying, with numbers that enhanced her Cancer Sun Sign. He was more yang, with a Sun Sign and numbers that enhanced his 7 researcher/accuracy trait. As a wedding gift, she asked me to walk through their home and give a few pieces of advice. I smiled as I walked from room to room saying "this is his room"—water reflective black, and metal, "this is her room"—wood furniture, family heirlooms, warm earth fabrics... reminder that I don't tap into the formal element of the Sun Sign (for instance) as much as the emotional aspect that supports it. Then we went into their bedroom—a wood bed, and furniture, they were painting the walls green, some splashes of low-key reds, a green comforter and sheets, no pictures yet (which was to be expected). I asked, "How do either of you sleep in here?" Her response was "Not well." Why? First, it wasn't a balanced room—all wood, a little earth, and a little fire. Plus she was over wooded, and he had no support at all for accuracy and career acceleration personality traits (involving metal, and some water elements like pictures with metal frames with real glass). What's interesting is the contemporary reflective black looks very nice with darker, comforting wood, and her new husband had asked if he could add those types of items. We are very intuitive beings (even those who don't claim to be).

The following is what each Astrology, Numerology, and Sun Sign connect with on an emotional level. This is the way I utilize it (many times), but remember that you can revise this chart to your liking (even add air if it suits you). These do change when you have traits that accelerate/intensify, decelerate/lessen, neutralize, compliment.

As far as the elements relating to the masculine and feminine:

Depending on the flow of the water (rapids versus babbling brook), you will receive varying energy results. Rapid is more yang, and babbling more ying and soothing as a general rule.

Wood would be softer, ying.

Metal would be a sharper, more accurate, yang.

Earth (the mother) would be more ying.

Fire, even in its calmest state, would be yang.

However, your intention and life experiences are very important. If someone beat you over the head with a wooden stick regularly, wood may not be soft, calm, and ying. But the concept of balancing the elements is like becoming one with nature, mountains, rocks, trees, plants, soil, the sun, and streams. To detailed astrologers, and feng shui fans, these do not exactly match your studies, as the concepts are based on how the elements connect with BMP personalities and emotions. Remember that with anything you study, allow yourself some time to absorb information then tidy up your truth in whatever fashion fits for you (research, intuition, generalizations...).

To further explain my choices, I provide words within the following chart (starting on the next page). Each trait has a bit of every element, but my intention is to identify what I have observed to be more dominant qualities in connection with BMP.

	Changing & Flowing **Water** Activity	Healthy & Comforting **Wood** Activity	Wise & Accurate **Metal** Activity	Grounded & Serene **Earth** Activity	Rapid Vibration **Fire** Activity
ARIES *(FIRE)*		Charm			Impulsively Lead
TAURUS *(EARTH)*		Responsible, Patient		Comfort	
GEMINI *(AIR)*	Newness (yang)				Jane of all trades, Fickle
CANCER *(WATER)*	Instinctive, Moody (ying)	Comforter		Protect people/ things love	
LEO *(FIRE)*		Love of Community, Generous			Vibrant, Attract Attention
VIRGO *(EARTH)*			Detailed	Healer	
LIBRA *(AIR)*		Balance, Harmony			Companionship, Please others
SCORPIO *(WATER)*			Strategic Analyzer		Inner Passion, Intense

	Water	Wood	Metal	Earth	Fire
SAGITTARIUS *(FIRE)	Freedom Seeker (ying)				Indulgent, Networker
CAPRICORN *(EARTH)			Calculating, Disciplined	Climber, Builder	
AQUARIUS *(AIR)	Out-of-the-box (ying)	Faith in people			Noticeably rebellious
PISCES *(WATER)	Intuitive (ying)			Faith	
*(element) acknowledges the Astrology element but not necessarily connected to BMP emotional elements.					
#1	Control (yang)				Lead
#2		Listen	Selectively Detailed Creativity		
#3	Ever-expanding (yang)				Free to Communicate
#4		Loyal		Build Foundation	
#5	Constant Ideas (noisy yang)				Free, Multi-tasker
#6		Server		Community	

	Water	Wood	Metal	Earth	Fire
#7			Analysis		Guarded
#8	Redirecting the flow (yang)				Monetary Flow
#9		Harmony		Commitment	
#11	Intuitive (ying)			Faith	
#22	Ever expanding (ying and yang)	Harmony		Comfort	Achievement
#33		Uplifting		Wise Seeker	
FIRST BORN	Control (yang)		Organized, Accurate		
ONLY	Control (yang)		Research		Independent
MIDDLE		Negotiator		Realist	
YOUNGEST	Charmer (ying)				Outgoing

The point of this exercise is that you've identified a Birth Mix Pattern (true inner self, cosmic DNA), and to go deeper look to external influences as well. Understand how your external environment supports you—your bedroom (where you lay your head every night), your eating area (is it healthy?), your work/creation space (does it express you?). For those you are in relationship with, go into the spaces that they consider sacred, and supportive (or not so) and this will tell you a great deal about their current states (especially with an awareness of their BMP). Also consider symbols—pictures, words, books, other messages—are they positive or negative, do they nurture or not?

Please, please, please (did I say please?) take this information in stride. Allow your intuition and training to identify elements if you have other opinions. But guaranteed, you will be able to understand positive and negative influences for yourself and others by paying attention to the external in conjunction with the internal BMP.

So let's go onto the Astrology, Numerology, and Birth Order details.

IV. Birth Mix Patterns

Calculating Astrology, Numerology, and Birth Order

You've seen pieces of the following information in my other books. I provide this type of information consistently throughout the *Birth Mix Patterns* series so that each book is content rich and you get an immediate understanding of the concepts and how to use them.

You'll also notice that each BMP book has its own personality. One analyzes hundreds of historic figures and lists famous people for each Astrology, Numerology and Birth Order topic. Another analyzes how groups interact utilizing the Birth Mix Patterns process. And this book (the third in the Birth Mix Patterns series) looks at love relationships and introduced visual grids to help visualize why people are interacting positively and negatively. All my available books published to date are found in the "About the Author" section and you can go to www.MichellePayton.com for updates. Use the following to understand how to calculate Birth Mix Patterns utilizing Astrology, Numerology, and Birth Order.

Astrology Sun Signs

BMP connects to the day and month of birth only (time, place, and year are not factors for this exercise). The sun is the core of the solar system, and sustains all other planets. While more intricate Astrology provides much more detail (including more planets), BMP focuses on our core of being, the ruling planet in our Astrology chart, the planet where we are most likely to come to terms with our true selves, and happiness.

For more details, go to Section V in this reference book on Astrology.

Numerology Life Path Number

This is connected to the day, month and year of birth and is one of the most important calculations in a Numerology chart. It summarizes your life—the challenges, karma, lessons and general personality trends. More intricate Numerology utilizes the letters of your birth name, as well as current name. Calculate Life Path as follows:

August 15, 1963 → Get each to lowest denominator (1-9, 11, 22 or 33):

8 (August month of birth)

15 (day of birth) → 1+5=6

1963 (year of birth) → 1+9+6+3=19; 1+9=10; 1+0=1

Final number: 8+6+1=15; 1+5=6 Life Path.

If any of the three numbers being calculated are 11, 22, or 33 then this would be the lowest denominator. The final number will be 1-9, 11, 22 or 33. For instance:

November 29, 1802

11 (month of birth) → 11 (lowest denominator)

29 (day of birth) → 2+9=11 (lowest denominator)

1802 (year of birth) → 1+8+0+2=11 (lowest denominator)

Final number: 11+11+11=33 Life Path (lowest denominator)

This is also referred to as Life Path 33/6, depending on the free will choices of the individual.

A note on the above Numerology examples. When double, or triple numbers are in a Numerology mix, this intensifies the number. It either intensifies functionally (expressing the positive side of the personality), or dysfunctionally (expressing the negative). More on this on the acceleration points section.

NUMEROLOGY MAJOR AND MINOR SUB-LESSONS

Sub-lesson numbers show additional life lessons within your path, and is connected to your day of birth. For instance:

August 15, 1963 equals:

15 (day of birth) → 1+5=6;

The major sub-lesson is 1+5=6;

The minor sub-lessons are 1, and 5.

With this particular birth date, the Life Path is 6, with a major sub-lesson of 6, and minor sub-lessons of 1, and 5. To further demonstrate the weight, or value of the lessons, say you have $20, $10, and $5 bills. The more money you have the higher gain in your personality mix. The Life Path is your $20 (your highest gain). The major sub-lesson is $10 (additional ways to manifest). The minor sub-lesson(s) is $5 (a bit more to manifest).

Birth Order

This is connected to the order of birth, and role you played out within the family unit that raised you from infancy, and beyond. There are differing opinions on Birth Order theories. The following makes most sense when applying to my life experiences and observations. It can be intricate as it takes into account years between births, gender, physical/mental strengths, and weaknesses (handicaps, body build, physical attractiveness, intellect), size of family, adoption…

There are rules of thumb that a variety of experts embrace, and have helped me in my baseline work:

If the siblings are both five years or more older and younger than you (and/or no other siblings are below, or above you), you can take on Only child traits.

If you are second in birth line, but the sibling above you is of opposite gender, you are also First Born, but of the opposite gender, and can take on First Born patterns.

If you are second in birth line but the sibling above you is handicapped, if you have problems with physical attractiveness, body build, or other perceived weaker qualities you may take on the traits of First Born (switching Birth Order in essence).

If you are from a large family, the family units can run in fours—First Born number one and fourth born is Youngest.

Middle children are not always predictable. They can be the pleasers, or the rebels, but generally are negotiators.

Adopted children can become rebellious at any order (ownership factors), and birth dates are not always accurate to get a full baseline.

There are always exceptions to these rules and many, many, many opinions.

Acceleration Points

This is when one, or more of the birth mix elements (Astrology, Numerology, and Birth Order) accelerate a particular personality theme or pattern. These can become life strengths, or challenges. For instance, a Leo can be very generous, Life Path 6 takes care of people, and First Born is the boss and, sometimes, organizer, caregiver, or parent of younger siblings. In this instance, the challenge is to not become an enabler by over caring (Leo, 6), and having money problems due to over generosity (Leo, 6). This combination can also result in being adored for being so giving (Leo, 6), and known for being reliable (First Born, 6).

When working strictly with the numbers, if the month, day, and/or year are the same number this indicates that personality traits intensify to the positive or negative. Intensity also increases adding zero at the end of numbers (like 10, 20, and 30).

Birth Mix Patterns: Explaining the Explanations

Astrology, Numerology, and Birth Order references used in the BMP (Birth Mix Patterns) tables, include the following terms:

PERSONALITY THEME, OR PATTERN:
What inspires you at the core, and pushes you in a particular direction

ROLE:
An acting out of your theme

BEST AT:
Your strengths

CHALLENGES:

Your personality diamonds in the rough that bring you to a higher consciousness of who you are as you expand, expect some of these to become new strengths, and personal developments

F: Financial Expression

I: Intellectual Expression

P: Physical Expression

So: Social Expression

Sp: Spiritual Expression

BMP SUMMARY:

A summary of the information provided in regards to theme, role, best at, and challenges, plus additional commentary on how this relates to the specific person, and/or event discussed, and/or how this relates to financial, intellectual, physical, social, and/or spiritual development

NUMEROLOGY PERSONAL YEARS

Personal Year is based on your birth day and month and the current year as a calculation and gives you a feel for the energy that surrounds you during that calendar year (contemplative, planning, clearing). There are nine (9) Personal Year numbers to complete a growth cycle. You calculate it as follows:

August 15, 2007

$2007 = 2 + 0 + 0 + 7 = 9$ (current year)

$8 = 8$ (month)

$15 = 1 + 5 = 6$ (day)

so: $8 + 6 + 9 = 23$; $2 + 3 = 5$ Personal Year.

The lowest denominator for Personal Year calculation is 1-9.

V. Your Birth Mix Pattern: Astrology, Numerology, and Birth Order Personality Traits

Astrology Sun Sign Influences

Astrology in its simplest terms is taking a snapshot of the position of the planets in the Earth's solar system on the date and time of your birth to understand your personality patterns, life themes, future, and more. There are endless pieces of information that you can extrapolate through Astrology, but with this BMP process, we will only focus on the Sun Sign. This is the object that all planets revolve around as a result of its life giving capabilities. It is our biggest personality influence.

Notice that we begin with March (around Spring Equinox). This is the Earth's new year (rebirthing), the season of new beginnings. The following are short summaries of each Sun Sign to identify your own patterns, as well as others.

ARIES (RAM): MARCH 21ST-APRIL 20TH
THE CHARMING ACHIEVER

Personality Theme: To be admirably first.

Role: Inspiring leader.

Best at (on good days): Being assertive. Generating ideas. Moving on impulse/intuition.

Challenges (on bad days): Changing on the Aries terms. Being temperamental, not patient, and curt. Finishing, focusing, and specializing.

F.I.P.S.S. (FINANCIAL, INTELLECTUAL, PHYSICAL, SOCIAL, SPIRITUAL):

F—Strong when control impulsive behavior. Can make money, but holding onto can be difficult.

I—Strong when structured enough to become an expert or specialist.

P—Strong when decreases leaping before looking and slows down (focus on one process for health regiment).

So—Strong when perceives being in front. Stronger when values others' ideas/thoughts.

Sp—Strong when not perceived being forced into an idea or told what to do.

ARIES BMP SUMMARY:

Focusing, and finishing what is started enhances the Aries life experience. If you're not able to do this individually, find a "finishing" team (and keep it positive, show tolerance, and listen to ideas). Obtain structured learning so that communication intending to be inspirational has substance for the listener.

Taurus (Bull): April 20ᵀᴴ-May 21ˢᵀ
The Stabilizer

Personality Theme: The calm in the midst of any storm. Creates solid homes, friends, jobs, marriages, and children.

Role: Always there for you. Secure and stable (less impulsive).

Best at (on good days): Being there for long-term, honesty.

Challenges (on bad days): Being lazy, stubborn, too comfortable, money hungry, or complacent.

F.I.P.S.S. (Financial, Intellectual, Physical, Social, Spiritual):

F—Strong when overcome need to hoard money and earthly possessions. One of the reasons why great providers, is seek long-term stability.

I—Strong when near (comfortable) home (or what feels like home) on a regular basis.

P—Strong when beat habit of gaining weight (comfort food). Important to keep balanced foods, drinks… as lifestyle.

So—Strong when secure and comfortable.

Sp—Strong when achieves harmony with Earth and spirit.

Taurus BMP Summary:

When functional, the Taurus is a great friend, guardian, and life partner. There are $50 chairs, and $5000 chairs, and both are comfortable. Being too hooked on possessions can create an unproductive, disappointing life for a Taurus. Frame perceptions as positive (find the silver linings), and Taurus will thrive!

Gemini (Twins): May 21ˢᵗ-June 22ⁿᵈ
The Witty Change Agent

Personality Theme: Trying new things. Being clever, communicating strategically yet artistically.

Role: Communicating like it's an art form. Make out-of-the-box changes because you can.

Best at (on good days): Being clever, witty communicators, multi-tasking.

Challenges (on bad days): Staying interested in anything, or anyone long-term. Slowing down, and being in the moment. Focusing.

F.I.P.S.S. (Financial, Intellectual, Physical, Social, Spiritual):

F—Strong when balance bank account/budget. Tend to be interested in new technology, ideas, products.

I—Strong when can explore, play with, experience many new technology options, events happening, developments, ideas, places.

P—Strong when can decrease mind noise through physical movement.

So—Strong when overcomes fickle nature for more long-term, inner circle relationships to develop (have many acquaintances).

Sp—Strong when subject is interesting enough.

Gemini BMP Summary:

New technology, communication enhancers, and people are exciting. Utilizing communication in a way that is positive for all parties is a win:win. Fickle behavior is short-sighted, and loss in many forms can result (financially, intellectually, physically, socially, and spiritually). Mastering a subject with multi-facets will keep the Gemini's interest.

CANCER (CRAB): JUNE 22ND-JULY 23RD
THE COMFORTER

Personality Theme: Cosmic Mothers and Fathers.

Role: Nurturers. Empathizers.

Best at (on good days): Being dependable. Being intuitive, and sensitive to change, and (as a result) being great visionaries.

Challenges (on bad days): Smothering those they care about. Hanging on too tightly to events, people, things (including money). Not feeling safe to show true emotions.

F.I.P.S.S. (FINANCIAL, INTELLECTUAL, PHYSICAL, SOCIAL, SPIRITUAL):

F—Strong when using empathy skills, and can be cutting edge on any front as a result. Rarely without money as have tendency to hold it tightly.

I—Strong when have someone in life to share knowledge, travel, expansion with.

P—Strong when limit comfort food. Important to notice how feel when eat certain products.

So—Strong when nurturing but can form dependence if too nurturing and create opposite effect resulting in people avoiding Cancers.

Sp—Strong when comforted and nurtured.

CANCER BMP SUMMARY:

Hanging on to things and people due to insecurity creates unhappiness for all involved. Allow the feminine moon energy to glow, feel warm, and welcoming, and others will find the way to the Cancer mother/father to be nurtured.

Leo (Lion): July 23ʀᴅ-August 22ɴᴅ
The Leader of the Pride

Personality Theme: Being in the spotlight. Establishing a pride—community, group, or circle.

Role: To take care of the pride—circle of friends, family, business. To lead, and shine.

Best at (on good days): Outward self-expression, creativity, and willpower.

Challenges (on bad days): Being self-absorbed. Being overly generous as result of taking care of the pride—circle of friends, family, community, business.

F.I.P.S.S. (Financial, Intellectual, Physical, Social, Spiritual):

F—Strong when image is not a self-centered ruler. Balance physical with realistic financial situation.

I—Strong when personal image is healthy, and no limits to expanding knowledge.

P—Strong when temptation to be lazy doesn't take over. Usually being healthy completes the sought after image.

So—Strong when doesn't expect a return for generosity, and doesn't keep score.

Sp—Strong when limelight is less important than connecting to spirit.

Leo BMP Summary:

There are many ways to care for "the pride." Be entertaining, fun, delightful, and generous with time more so than money, so that finances are balanced. The outward expression (physical appearance) is part of Leo creativity, and are symbols stating well-being. Express this within financial means.

VIRGO (VIRGIN): AUGUST 22^(ND)-SEPTEMBER 22^(ND)
THE DETAILED CONSTANT EXPANDER

Personality Theme: Serving the greater good. Seeking detailed order. Constant self-improvement.

Role: Worker bee. Organizer, and Analyzer (on own detailed terms).

Best at (on good days): Helping, organizing, analyzing and efficiently fixing things on own detailed terms—knowing where everything is, even when observers perceive disorganization.

Challenges (on bad days): Letting the mind, body, and spirit relax in the moment as opposed to constantly improving and analyzing the details.

F.I.P.S.S. (FINANCIAL, INTELLECTUAL, PHYSICAL, SOCIAL, SPIRITUAL):

F—Strong when can improve, dig into details and be the influencer of the outcome.

I—Strong when studies/travel allows for learning that can be perfected and put into practice.

P—Strong when decrease stress of being too detailed. Tend to need clear benefits and details of what is truly healthy in order to fully embrace.

So—Strong when move past the idea that all relationships have to be perfect. Allow for play time.

Sp—Strong when enough information is gathered that points to being on the best path. Some have a major connection to Earth and plants— particularly those that have a clear healing purpose.

VIRGO BMP SUMMARY:

Virgos are great at details. They do this to be credibly helpful. Using research as enhancers/expanders versus controls/weapons will help this sign maintain healthy bodies (not stressing over the small stuff), and relationships—personally, and professionally. For the same reasons (health/relationship), get more detailed on how to play.

LIBRA (SCALES): SEPTEMBER 22ND-OCTOBER 23RD
THE BALANCER

Personality Theme: Strives for balance, and harmony in all things.

Role: Joining/Restoring both sides/halves with the ultimate goal of achieving beauty, and harmony.

Best at (on good days): Manifesting beauty (often expressed with the arts), charm, socializing, pacifying.

Challenge (on bad days): Being decisive. Unrealistically looking for perfection in all things.

F.I.P.S.S. (FINANCIAL, INTELLECTUAL, PHYSICAL, SOCIAL, SPIRITUAL):

F—Strong when sees immediate return and connection with beauty, harmony, perfection.

I—Strong when able to travel and study the arts.

P—Strong when inner thoughts match outer beauty, perfection, and charm—physical surroundings as well as body.

So—Strong when being admired and can share beauty, harmony, perfection vision with others.

Sp—Strong when is immediately obvious that overall perfection, harmony can be achieved.

LIBRA BMP SUMMARY:

With the Libra job description also including "to restore balance," a tough transition on this path is to grasp that the situation as already perfect. To find the perfection, and beauty in imperfection, increases abilities to comfortably, and confidently make the smallest to the largest of decisions. Recognize that you are only in control of your actions. Provide information others will hear when they are ready, then let go of the rest for soul sanity.

SCORPIO (SCORPION): OCTOBER 23RD-NOVEMBER 22ND
THE PATIENT ACHIEVER

Personality Theme: Keeping everything and everyone in line.

Role: In control.

Best at (on good days): Being patient while inwardly maintaining passion and commitment.

Challenges (on bad days): Sharing feelings. Can be intense and need a lot of space when processing. Feelings get hurt easily, and has difficulty forgiving and forgetting.

F.I.P.S.S. (FINANCIAL, INTELLECTUAL, PHYSICAL, SOCIAL, SPIRITUAL):

F—Strong when given opportunity as excels with any job. Savers of money.

I—Strong when phenomena or puzzles to be solved, concepts to be molded. Very strategic.

P—Strong when let go of anger/resentments (sometimes accelerates to revenge). Must achieve to be fully physically well.

So—Strong when can outwardly express feelings, and when allowing others to freely express without judgment or resentment.

Sp—Strong when embrace the concept of faith and see value in being happy.

Scorpio BMP Summary:

Scorpio's can be perceived as mysterious, shy, or quiet. Being alone to process is a necessity for many Scorpios. However, loved ones can be of help, if Scorpios allow it. When inward processing sessions are complete, the Scorpio must let go of the belief that others have done wrong (sometimes then seeking revenge). Otherwise, living in the past, results in never knowing what one truly has (what is making one happy) in the present, and will be a constant burden that may even express itself as physical ailments. Communicate with care, truth, respect, and love once matters are processed independently.

Sagittarius (Archer): November 22ND-December 22ND
The Life Partaker

Personality Theme: Combining fun and freedom to the journey to eventually find the meaning of life that unites everyone (or many key people).

Role: Life of the party (of a large admiring audience). Networker—makes sure knows key people.

Best at (on good days): Adjusting to changes in scenery and life situations. Idea generation.

Challenges (on bad days): Complete commitment (calming the stallion) and attention to detail.

F.I.P.S.S. (Financial, Intellectual, Physical, Social, Spiritual):

F—Strong when resources are available—especially others' resources. Growth likely when accompanied by focus.

I—Strong when creative expression allowed.

P—Strong when learn to slow down and focus.

So—Strong when have audience (party people). Over time will enrich life when differentiate party and inner circles.

Sp—Strong when doesn't interfere with freedom.

SAGITTARIUS **BMP** SUMMARY:

Creative freedom fuels the Sag soul. If this is not the Sag reality (no longer fun), then jobs (and the finances), relationships, or projects may all be considered a jail sentence to this Sun Sign. Addictions (in various forms) can become an issue. Buckle down, and focus on something that will keep your interest for the long-term. However, you will only be happy if adventure and variety is in your mix. It's tempting to go for the quick fixes, but less likely to work for you and decreases any possible stability so you can continue to play in style.

CAPRICORN (GOAT): DECEMBER 22ND-JANUARY 21ST
THE CLIMBER

Personality Theme: The "One" in ultimate control and power of themselves and others.

Role: Ambitious and goal-oriented to build something that will last (stable). Willing to move slowly to reach the fullest power potential.

Best at (on good days): Manifesting success through slow, organized, calculated methods. Patience. Helping build a situation, society, event that serves the masses. Creating foundation.

Challenge (on bad days): Positively remembering the people that sponsored success, and not always linking relationships to power and position. Being okay that it can be lonely at the top, when leadership style is aggressive—may require overcoming tendency to be cold, rigid, or suspicious if feeling position is threatened.

F.I.P.S.S. (Financial, Intellectual, Physical, Social, Spiritual):

F—Strong when creates a solid foundation. Reaches the top of many fields and money is (many times) the key to getting there.

I—Strong when study/travel gains leadership/power position.

P—Strong when keep pessimism low so body will not absorb negativity.

So—Strong and stable when view alliances, friends, and inner circle relationships as long-term (versus here today, gone tomorrow). Important to balance need for power and authority with kindness.

Sp—Strong when creates comfort, warmth and security and compatible with leadership goals.

Capricorn BMP Summary:

It's healthier to acknowledge that being a successful leader, authority, or accomplished—in your chosen social, family and/or business associations—is who you are. Understanding how to relax and integrate being genuine while building, leading, organizing, or setting rules can create a positive, long-term network of relationships.

Aquarius (Water Bearer): January 21st-February 19th
Out-of-the-Box

Personality Theme: Diverse, out-of-the-box trend detectives and setters.

Role: Open-minded—sometimes considered eccentric—change agents (but stubbornly firm once ideas are "truth").

Best at (on good days): Manifesting ideas well before their time—not limited to one area of expertise, or current truth. Seeing past self, and more toward masses. Being social.

Challenges (on bad days): Being bored and detached. Can be very social, but connecting with individuals can sometimes be a chore when consumed with innovation. Rebellious.

F.I.P.S.S. (Financial, Intellectual, Physical, Social, Spiritual):

F—Strong when work with cutting edge (includes arts, sciences...) and manage tendency to overextend in various ways.

I—Strong when able to study creative, out-of-the-box, intellectual ideal concepts, causes and places.

P—Strong when exercise as grounds in the physical and feels like part of this world. Tendency to be attractive and coordinated.

So—Strong when doesn't sacrifice relationships for higher good (can detach to achieve the "good"). Very giving and will open home to anyone for sake of overall humanity. Generally likeable.

Sp—Strong when connecting to causes—the higher good, diversity and overall humanity.

Aquarius BMP Summary:

Priding yourself on being so out-of-the-box, at times, creates a feeling of not being of this world—sometimes you may feel this way, sometimes others see you this way. There's a healthy balance that comes in socializing and stepping into others' energies (who love you, who provide social outlets, who take you outside of work/creating) to connect with the mainstream world. The secret to increasing creative, out-of-the-box expression is allowing the mind to rest, be playful, be loving, and loveable. This also increases physical, and non-physical productivity.

Pisces (Fishes): February 19ᵗʰ-March 21ˢᵗ
The Intuitive Visualizer

Personality Theme: Believing in, and understanding others. Having faith.

Role: Intuitive/Heightened sensitive. Spiritual motivator and visualizer.

Best at (on good days): Bringing others to higher levels through listening, compassion, sympathy, and empathy, while effectively protecting yourself from psychic over-stimulation of others.

Challenges (on bad days): Taking on others' feelings as own. Being realistic. Connecting to the physical world.

F.I.P.S.S. (Financial, Intellectual, Physical, Social, Spiritual):

F—Strong when intuitive hunches are practical and finances are carefully managed. Many prefer behind the scenes work.

I—Strong when study/travel can apply to real-life education, and most fun when can combine dreamy/imaginary and real worlds.

P—Strong when can manage tendency to overindulge. High sensitivity to environment, food, drink, drugs, sugar and bad doses of other people.

So—Strong when have a special physical space to share with inner circle friends. At times prefer to be alone and even hide from the world (especially if hurt by those trusted in past).

Sp—Strong when understands self as much as others, and has faith in own intuition.

Pisces BMP Summary:

Grounding is a must to live in the physical world (for physical self preservation—having food, shelter, and clothing). Get training/education so that (many) jobs are easy to attain. There will be times when mixing with the mainstream world feels uncomfortable, so consider professional and personal environments that provide options to psychically protect yourself. Develop tools (protection techniques) to guard from emotional/psychic vampires (the weak who must feed off of others to gain satisfaction). Know, above all else, that your "feelings" lead to the path of least resistance. You don't necessarily need to know all the details to have faith.

Numerology Life Path, Major, and Minor Sub-Lessons Influences

Numerology in its simplest terms is using numbers to understand your personality patterns and life themes. This can be done by using the numbers associated with your birth date, and assigning numbers to the letters in your name. There are endless pieces of information that can be extrapolated from the numbers, but we will only focus on the numbers that quickly serve as a personality summary.

We'll look at numbers 1 through 9, 11, 22, and 33. The following summarizes the patterns of each number so you can identify your own and others' patterns:

LIFE PATH 1: THE LEADER

Personality Theme: Being ahead. Do it better and faster. Seek finer things.

Role: Provider. Leader.

Best at (on good days): Being own boss.

Challenges (on bad days): Taking orders from others. Following. Finding value in listening.

F.I.P.S.S. (FINANCIAL, INTELLECTUAL, PHYSICAL, SOCIAL, SPIRITUAL):

F—Strong when can demonstrate management skills and has control. Hard work is expression of status.

I—Strong when can express pioneer spirit and fulfill goals.

P—Strong when maintain food/exercise program as this physical accomplishment demonstrates ability to lead. Many enjoy competitive activities to stay in shape.

So—Strong when connects with others—hears their opinions and is less self-absorbed.

Sp—Strong when learns to appreciate life overall and less for appearance.

1 BMP SUMMARY:

The 1 can be obsessed with pushing ahead, and is very competitive in all areas of life. Relaxing past the drive is good for a 1's health. The 1 will likely be in a state of more complete happiness when physical accomplishments are balanced with a spiritual sense.

LIFE PATH 2: THE INWARD CREATOR/MOTIVATOR

Personality Theme: The perfect tranquil environment.

Role: Counselor. The bringer of balance within diverse situations.

Best at (on good days): Team motivating. Listening. Inward creativity.

Challenges(on bad days): Overt leading. Fully expanding own talents as tend to hold back to serve others, and keep the peace.

F.I.P.S.S. (FINANCIAL, INTELLECTUAL, PHYSICAL, SOCIAL, SPIRITUAL):

F—Strong when can express perfectionist nature—possibly as a counselor, physical or massage therapist, hands-on healer, expressive creator, artist, author, communicator.

I—Strong when abilities are not underestimated by others.

P—Strong when overcomes pattern of gaining weight due to lack of self-involvement or excessive inward thinking. Balance lifestyle, combining realistic exercise while inwardly processing.

So—Strong when not as shy and can utilize diplomatic, tactful, sensitive, team player talents.

Sp—Strong when achieves harmonious internal and external environment. Great eye for beauty.

2 BMP Summary:

All love the 2's listening and team approaches. However, the 2 can be too diplomatic and miss opportunities. Openly communicating true thoughts (in 2's thoughtful way) is helpful to releasing frustration (and even physical weight), especially when unfairly underestimated.

Life Path 3: The Informed Speaker/Communicator

Personality Theme: Being informed. Being respected as a result of being informed. Being heard.

Role: The expert and/or informer to inspire others.

Best at (on good days): Sharing information. Executing as a result of being well-informed, but requires focus/education.

Challenge (on bad days): So busy at being informed, and informing, may prefer not to do detailed processes of running daily life.

F.I.P.S.S. (Financial, Intellectual, Physical, Social, Spiritual):

F—Strong when takes life seriously, works hard and focuses. Many times are writers, poets, musicians at an early age.

I—Strong when allowed to express self freely.

P—Strong when can apply discipline to the fun-loving, free attitude.

So—Strong when develops listening skills (particularly with inner circle) but known to be a social butterfly. Has many acquaintances and
generous to a fault.

Sp—Strong when decides to focus. Important not to take self too seriously to achieve happiness.

3 BMP Summary:

The 3's can be frustrated, even angry, if perceived they're not being "heard."
It's important to focus, listen, study, and become an expert in something
(or two, or three) so people can see and acknowledge the 3's value.

Life Path 4: The Realist, Problem Solver, Builder of Order

Personality Theme: Create order. Create method and process to overcome
life challenges—sometimes physical, or emotional.

Role: Problem Solver. Hard Worker. Establish foundation.

Best at (on good days): Making decisions, organizing, persevering, being
detailed and dependable.

Challenges (on bad days): Scattering energy too far to solve too many
problems at one time. Being too rigid, or dogmatic. Taking a lot
longer to learn a lesson because has to experience on own (can't take
others' word).

F.I.P.S.S. (Financial, Intellectual, Physical, Social, Spiritual):

F—Strong when energy is focused (not scattered and chaotic) and can
express precision, discipline, method, order. Not afraid to work and
put in long hours to build career, nest egg and can handle money

carefully but can miss opportunities if too cautious and detailed (by missing the big picture).

I—Strong when working with conventional ideas. Stronger when flexible in thinking and open to new ideas.

P—Strong when not overworking and apply same focus to health.

So—Strong when able to demonstrate their reliability, dependability, and loyalty. Great parent, life partner, friend.

Sp—Strong when process is clear. Personal growth hinges on ability to judge less harshly—being flexible with opposing ideas.

4 BMP SUMMARY:

The 4 is loved for loyalty. The 4 can be too set in established processes (it's comfortable there). Increase physical and mental flexibility—yoga, drive a different way home, begin shopping in different areas of the grocery store. This creates a more relaxed, playful, adventurous 4.

LIFE PATH 5: THE UNENDING TALENT

Personality Theme: New experiences. Change. New Ideas. Freedom.

Role: Change Agent. Out-of-the-box on their terms.

Best at (on good days): Brainstorming. Innovating. Multi-tasking.

Challenges (on bad days): Focus and finishing due to so many ideas, and overall talent. Sometimes quality suffers.

F.I.P.S.S. (FINANCIAL, INTELLECTUAL, PHYSICAL, SOCIAL, SPIRITUAL):

F—Strong when regularly experience new ideas, concepts and people. Great in sales, advertising, PR, politics, self-employment as long as stick to becoming an expert in a few areas rather than mastering none.

I—Strong when can experience/partake in all areas of life. Travel and adventure high on goal list.

P—Strong when disciplined on controlling food and other substance intake (too much adventure). Keep the body limber to match your limber/flexible (new, free, change) ideas.

So—Strong when feeling free to experience adventure, travel, variety.

Sp—Strong when not forced into conventional thought. Being less intense brings inner harmony.

5 BMP SUMMARY:

Boredom is the worst for a 5. Prioritizing, focusing, and finishing what you start (not just crossing off your task list, but doing it completely, and well) will enhance life experiences. Find ways to make the journey as satisfying as the completion—includes jobs, tasks, and relationships. Enjoy the new, and appreciate the established.

LIFE PATH 6: THE RESPONSIBLE ONE/THE SERVER

Personality Theme: Serving others. Compassionate.

Role: Cosmic Mother or Father. Organizer to help others accomplish goals/heal.

Best at (on good days): Leading charismatically and reliably.

Challenges (on bad days): Interfering or saving others too much. Creatively expressing him/herself fully. Over-tasking.

F.I.P.S.S. (FINANCIAL, INTELLECTUAL, PHYSICAL, SOCIAL, SPIRITUAL):

F—Strong when develop reliable tools to help others and can utilize personal charm and charisma to create success in business, organizations and events.

I—Strong when connected to personal growth as well as need to serve others.

P—Strong when control cravings for dairy and sweets. Generally graceful and attractive.

So—Strong when express counseling side functionally versus controlling. Accept love in return for service. Great life partner and parent.

Sp—Strong when overcome seeing self as "savior" (taking that weight off your shoulders) and thrive on spiritual returns as a result of kindness and generosity.

6 BMP SUMMARY:

Create the process then let go. People have to make their own mistakes to learn. It's possible to do for others without enabling, and have room for 6 creative outlets to live life to its fullest. When resentment develops, you've helped too much (and may be over-helping and enabling).

LIFE PATH 7: THE SOURCE OF KNOWLEDGE. EXPERT/THINKER/ANALYZER

Personality Theme: Absorbing vast amounts of information to become an expert.

Role: Utilizing or sharing knowledge to create clarity for others, self, and/or events.

Best at (on good days): Exploring, thinking, and putting the pieces together for "truth."

Challenges (on bad days): Being too guarded and self-centered. Not being open and trusting of others and their ideas.

F.I.P.S.S. (FINANCIAL, INTELLECTUAL, PHYSICAL, SOCIAL, SPIRITUAL):

F—Strong when expert information is useful to advancement.

I—Strong when have freedom to research independently, express (more linear) creativity and come up with practical solutions independently.

P—Strong when control cravings for physical pleasures.

So—Strong when open to others' ideas and overcome being too isolated, alone, independent. Can be very charming when centered but look to come out of the limelight rather quickly.

Sp—Strong as age (like good wine) and can be very connected with "spirituality."

7 BMP SUMMARY:

The 7 can over share due to the large amount of information you absorb. Give what the listener can handle, and your efforts will advance. Over sharing will result in people not listening to you. Under-sharing cheats the world from learning from you. Your knowledge can help many expand. Find that gentle, artful balance.

LIFE PATH 8: THE MATERIAL MANIFESTER

Personality Theme: Accumulate wealth. Create wealth.

Role: Manager. Visionary.

Best at (on good days): Manifesting money or other means when needed.

Challenges(on bad days): Holding onto wealth longer-term and effectively managing flow. Connecting to less material areas of life.

F.I.P.S.S. (FINANCIAL, INTELLECTUAL, PHYSICAL, SOCIAL, SPIRITUAL):

F—Strong when able to exercise long-range vision. Viewed as natural in business and management (politics, business, finance, law, science, manage large institutions) but can be greedy. Can have major highs and lows, but with awareness can manage more effectively.

I—Strong when travel and/or exposed to beautiful things. Being formally and informally educated is key to image.

P—Strong when in optimal shape—is a personal sign of success/ strength.

So—Strong when can be in a role to inspire and guide others. Can be pushy and arrogant decreasing positive relationships.

Sp—Strong when can connect with humanity and inner happiness and less with power and money.

8 BMP Summary:

Establish a baseline to manage the highs and lows of finances, employment, other physical manifestations, and long-range plans—spend this, save that, average levels are satisfactory at, make adjustments to accomplish goals. This makes it easier for the 8 to feel like inspiring others, rather than forcing 8 opinions (easier on all relationships at all levels). Be polite, and okay that not everyone needs, or wants to understand the big picture. Without the detail people, the 8 would complete little to nothing.

LIFE PATH 9: THE HUMANITARIAN

Personality Theme: A better world.

Role: Faith. Commitment.

Best at (on good days): Breaking ground where few others have the compassion to.

Challenges (on bad days): Balancing needs for physical rewards with spiritual. Can be too focused on dreams, and when not achieved can detach and may even blame others (feels victimized).

F.I.P.S.S. (FINANCIAL, INTELLECTUAL, PHYSICAL, SOCIAL, SPIRITUAL):

F—Strong when embrace the idea that material possessions are as much acquired as made (lucky investments, inheritances, others inspired by your work). Your network is key to your success. Find strategic loopholes to help your life flow with ease.

I—Strong when can focus on social impact and harmony. Great as interior and exterior design, socially conscious judge, minister, teacher, lawyer, environmentalist.

P—Strong when achieve overall fitness, which can be a mood balancer/ mind quieter—important when struggle with uncertainty and moodiness that pulls you down.

So—Strong when can be connected with variety of diverse people/situations. Tend to be less judgmental when achieve balance. Being too clingy to people and things can be a challenge.

Sp—Strong when can express philanthropist nature fully. May have additional connection with outdoors and animals.

9 BMP SUMMARY:

Be aware of and manage the internal struggle of money and overall harmony. Understand the 9 lives in a Universe of free will (as ALL do). Having the victim mentality (and swimming in others' dramas) is a challenge the 9 must move past to achieve true happiness. Take ownership in your choices, and have the courage to make new ones to create an easy flow (which could mean leaving certain people, places, and things behind). The 9 "succeeds," many times, as a result of being sponsored, and admired.

LIFE PATH 11: THE IN-THE-MOMENT INTUITIVE

Personality Theme: Maximizing the journey, and life experiences (highly charged "2").

Role: Seer, or Visionary.

Best at (on good days): Inventing in the moment (as life flows). Leading intuitively.

Challenges(on bad days): Grounding, and being practical with matters in the physical.

F.I.P.S.S. (FINANCIAL, INTELLECTUAL, PHYSICAL, SOCIAL, SPIRITUAL):

F—Strong when overcome being impractical. Need focus to realize full potential. Great inventors, artists, religious leaders, massage therapists, counselors, acupuncturists, or physical therapists.

I—Strong when confidence is high—very psychic and may not trust that. Likely to expand more with life experiences rather than formal education. Can be very critical of self.

P—Strong when able to balance diet and peaceful environment as an overall lifestyle and protect self from sensory overload from intuitive information.

So—Strong when can overcome withdrawn (at times perceived arrogant) nature as result of receiving intuitive messages. Perceptive to life partners and others' needs.

Sp—Strong when physically mature (by 30's to 40's). Can access information received over and above the obvious senses and connect with a higher source. May be seen as psychic.

11 BMP SUMMARY:

This is one of the more psychic numbers in Numerology. Trust your feelings. Because of the ability to "see," it can be challenging to be grounded in the physical. This is a great inventor, creator, intuitive arts number, but can be impractical. Train yourself how to manage money, and consider a structured education early in life to allow for professional flexibility.

Sensitivities are very high, so keep food balanced, and physical interactions balanced, including finding a system to protect yourself in crowds to minimize psychic overload.

LIFE PATH 22: THE MATERIAL AND HUMANITY MASTER

Personality Theme: Achieve ultimate financial and spiritual dreams (highly charged 4 builder/insightful 11).

Role: Committed to balance. Ambitious. Insightful. Methodical.

Best at (on good days): Breaking ground where no others could. Being self-confident.

Challenges (on bad days): Resting, and taking a back seat to the constant opportunities and projects that present themselves.

F.I.P.S.S. (FINANCIAL, INTELLECTUAL, PHYSICAL, SOCIAL, SPIRITUAL):

F—Strong when create method around insight to manifest dreams. Can over-extend energy and waste time chasing too many opportunities. Focus is key to manifestation.

I—Strong when have enough formal and informal training to fulfill dreams and express visions.

P—Strong when health doesn't take a back seat to material mastery. Stress is biggest challenge.

So—Strong when others can keep step with you (and not be intimidated) as you fulfill dreams.

Sp—Strong when surrender to the larger causes and are flexible as new information is introduced. Relaxing will increase internal peace.

22 BMP SUMMARY:

The 22 that focuses on a manageable number of opportunities at a time will be more likely to succeed. Formal and informal training, and allowing others to expand in the 22 success (and, in turn, they succeed) will fully expand this **Life Path** of humanity/spiritual, and material accomplishment. The bigger (and original) ideas may be hard to follow, and even be unbelievable. Give information in small doses to keep you, and your "team" from becoming frustrated. Help others take ownership in your goals so that they materialize.

LIFE PATH 33: THE SPIRITUAL TEACHER

Personality Theme: Spiritually uplifting to (wo)mankind (highly charged server 6).

Role: Devotion. Seeker of Understanding, and Wisdom. Judgment-Free.

Best at (on good days): Strong spiritual influence. Compassion.

Challenges (on bad days): Interfering, and enabling rather than helping.

F.I.P.S.S. (FINANCIAL, INTELLECTUAL, PHYSICAL, SOCIAL, SPIRITUAL):

F—Strong when develop reliable tools to help others and can utilize personal charm and charisma to create success in business, organizations and events.

I—Strong when connected to personal growth as well as need to serve others.

P—Strong when control cravings for dairy and sweets. Generally graceful and attractive.

So—Strong when express counseling side functionally versus controlling. Accept love in return for service.

Sp—Strong when thrive on spiritual returns as a result of your kindness and generosity.

33 BMP SUMMARY:

While tempting to always do for others, the 33 insight (to do things better, and faster) is balanced when allowing others to experience relative negatives and positives. Continue to be a resource, but allow others to experience their challenges on their own. This enhances their sense of accomplishments in this lifetime (and healing projects back to you as well).

Birth Order Influences

It's believed by some experts that we develop our Birth Order personality patterns by age two. Put in unscientific terms, Birth Order is a label each child psychologically owns within a family unit; First Born, Only, Middle, or Youngest. Unlike Astrology, and Numerology, where most agree on what Sun Sign, or Numerology numbers mean, there are a number of theories on the Birth Order concept. I have chosen to embrace the idea that there are no bad Birth Orders, simply opportunities to learn and expand to new levels.

The following summarizes patterns of each Birth Order so that you can identify your own patterns, as well as others:

FIRST BORN: THE ACHIEVER

Personality Theme: In control. The one in power.

Role: Ambitious, goal-oriented, conformist, responsible, organized.

Best at (on good days): Bringing people, projects, events together on time, following rules.

Challenges (on bad days): Being too controlling, and putting pressure on self and others to perform to First's expectations.

F.I.P.S.S. (FINANCIAL, INTELLECTUAL, PHYSICAL, SOCIAL, SPIRITUAL):

F—Strong when can be precise/detailed but able to think outside-of-the-box to establish new ideas/rules. Prefers to lead.

I—Strong when can collect facts and rules that can be established or followed.

P—Strong when looks like a leader (fit, lean, good looking), but if become too stressed "leading" can wear on the body.

So—Strong when overcome need to be too perfect and too demanding (decreases strain on relationships).

Sp—Strong when makes logical sense, and laws and rules are clear. Important to understand need to lighten up for inner health.

FIRST BORN BMP SUMMARY:

Precision is helpful. Effective, tolerant, supportive leading will go farther (in many instances). Listening to others' ideas, and entertaining new concepts will take the First far in personal, family, and business affairs. Demanding creates resentment even if it makes logical sense.

ONLY: THE TURBO ACHIEVER

Personality Theme: The Center of the World. Independent Creator.

Role: Goal-oriented, accumulator of knowledge, independent problem solver/creator.

Best at (on good days): Planning, setting, and reaching goals that clearly benefit the Only.

Challenges (on bad days): Seeing past the "Only" way.

F.I.P.S.S. (Financial, Intellectual, Physical, Social, Spiritual):

F—Strong when willing to rely on own abilities as opposed to being taken care of by others. Will sacrifice everything to succeed.

I—Strong when can collect facts.

P—Strong when looks like a leader (fit, lean, good looking) but if become too stressed "leading" can wear on the body (addictions can become an issue for escape).

So—Strong when receives attention. Most comfortable with older and younger friends. If understand how to put others first then develop more meaningful circles of friends.

Sp—Strong when makes logical sense and demonstrates clear personal benefits to self-fulfillment.

Only BMP Summary:

Achieving goals at any cost, may cost the Only dearly. Using facts to manipulate may work in the short-term until building loving, personal relationships becomes a goal as well. There are benefits to others being in the driver's seat.

Middle: The Negotiator

Personality Theme: Weaving own dreams with realism.

Role: Diplomat, negotiator, risk-taker, competitor (when larger family, can be less competitive).

Best at (on good days): Compromising. Making friends. Being flexible, and cooperative.

Challenges (on bad days): Not comfortable with confrontation (rather please others), but can be rebel, independent, stubborn, and/or secretive. Competitiveness varies.

F.I.P.S.S. (Financial, Intellectual, Physical, Social, Spiritual):

F—Strong when balance risk taking and generosity as a pleaser with creating future security.

I—Strong when focus on a course of study long enough. Life experiences and working with people is high intellectual stimulant.

P—Strong if social circle encourages fitness and/or if gets recognition/ seems special as a result of fitness.

So—Strong when feel like part of groups, events, clubs, teams. Loyal to friends and commitments but can be secretive and not ask for help if needed.

Sp—Strong when seen as a way to increase independent thinking. Important to fill social need.

Middle BMP Summary:

Middles can please some of the people some of the time. To always seek approval means Middles are not fully expressing their needs. It's time to get over parents' (perceived or real) lack of attention. The greatest learning of all is that being a part of a team is great fun, and rewarding. This is something the First Born sibling may be too serious to figure out (for a while, at least).

Youngest: The Charmer

Personality Theme: Enjoy life. Outgoing. Expressive.

Role: Fun, funny, people person, loving, and lovable.

Best at (on good days): Working with small groups, or one-on-one. Creative, innovative thinking, as they are more fun-loving, open, and feel less pressure to perform.

Challenges (on bad days): Listening. Being grown up. Following rules (question authority). Fitting into molds.

F.I.P.S.S. (Financial, Intellectual, Physical, Social, Spiritual):

F—Strong when figure out how to be a grown up and still express creativity and fun personality functionally. Great in sales.

I—Strong when turn natural ability to read people and situations into educational experience (formal education can be a challenge).

P—Strong when figure out how to discipline fun loving nature, food, drink, drugs, and sugar.

So—Strong when not seeking as much attention (natural entertainer) and can find more meaningful, reliable, inner circle.

Sp—Strong when can figure out how to balance being served with serving others.

Youngest BMP Summary:

Youngests can still be fun and successful at the same time. Take advantage of this Birth Order's natural ability to work well with people. Environments that are a bit more relaxed will maintain that likeable balance for you.

Personal Years

So we have your Birth Mix—Astrology, Numerology, Birth Order, and now Personal Year. This is based on your birth day and month and the current year as a calculation. This lasts for a full calendar year.

While I haven't given examples in the earlier case histories, this section will give you yet another example of how your energy is drawn in a particular direction to help you achieve your goals.

Personal Year 1: New Beginnings and Opportunities

Personal Year 1 Summary: You have just come off of a year of getting rid of everything that doesn't serve you. You were likely to cut out a bunch of karmic and physical clutter. If you didn't do this, you may spend, at least, the first part of this year making up for lost time. This is a Spring/Summer Vibration so you may see March through September being a major manifestation period for you, so hold onto your hat. However, don't expect to rock your world in six months' time. This is setting the ground work for future butt kicking. It's the little matters that end up adding up to bigger things over time. Some experiences in Year 1 could include:

PERSONAL YEAR 1: NEW BEGINNINGS AND OPPORTUNITIES

Year Theme: To make changes and birth new life ideas that set the tone for the next 9 years.

Role: To take control of your life to manifest the optimal reality.

Best at (on good days): Being renewed, new, active, changing.

Challenges (on bad days): Being calm and reflective enough to make decisions after coming off a purging year.

F.I.P.S.S. (FINANCIAL, INTELLECTUAL, PHYSICAL, SOCIAL, SPIRITUAL):

F—Strong time to change job, career, investment strategies which may require establishing a whole new set of rules.

I—Strong time to consider new learning paths and processes.

P—Strong time to consistently move your physical body and visualize being fit for the rest of your life.

So—Strong time to only keep relationships in your life that move you forward.

Sp—Strong time to decide on your rituals and ceremonies and practice them.

PERSONAL YEAR 2: PATIENCE AND TACT

PERSONAL YEAR 2 SUMMARY: Year 2 has a strong energy supporting introverted development. This doesn't mean that you won't be physically fit or successful in all that you set your sights on. It may, however, mean that your approach to all areas of life may be processed a bit more internally and slowly. If anything threatens your inner development it may trigger insecurities. For instance, if an idea isn't fully developed, you may feel like others will try to steal your concept (could be true or perceived). Patience is the key and unveiling at a specific (even calculated) time may be more important to you in this particular year. Some experiences in Year 2 could be:

PERSONAL YEAR 2: PATIENCE AND TACT

Year Theme: To quietly create.

Role: To be patient, influencing through tact, compromise and cooperation.

Best at (on good days): Advancing plans slowly and allowing things to unfold.

Challenges (on bad days): Perceiving situations as struggles rather than opportunities.

F.I.P.S.S. (FINANCIAL, INTELLECTUAL, PHYSICAL, SOCIAL, SPIRITUAL):

F—Strong time to observe and gently and patiently execute money and career strategies.

I—Strong time to read and research. Less of a pull of energy for travel unless connected with learning/study.

P—Strong time to observe physical set backs as opportunity to stretch (gently) to next level.

So—Strong time to focus on inner circle relationships. Good time for more meaningful interactions.

Sp—Strong time to go within, get quiet, rest within.

PERSONAL YEAR 3: SOCIAL AND LIGHTHEARTED

PERSONAL YEAR 3 SUMMARY: Year 3 is high energy and fun. It's faster paced than last year. Match this with summer cycle and you're going to feel turbo charged! You've come off of a very reflective year and things that seemed to take forever in your 2 Year, now seem almost effortless in comparison as long as you can focus. Some experiences in Year 3 could be:

PERSONAL YEAR 3: SOCIAL AND LIGHT HEARTED

Year Theme: To creatively expand.

Role: To socialize, create with high energy, and have fun.

Best at (on good days): High activity.

Challenges (on bad days): Lacking direction and discipline.

F.I.P.S.S. (FINANCIAL, INTELLECTUAL, PHYSICAL, SOCIAL, SPIRITUAL):

F—Strong time to have fun in your job, career, and enjoy solid finances but must apply some discipline.

I—Strong time to let go and enjoy life experiences. Free flow learning may include additional travel.

P—Strong time for high physical energy which can help keep body fit.

So—Strong time to meet new and exciting people—careful on empty relationships.

Sp—Strong challenge to quiet mind. Creatively combining physical fitness with spiritual approach may be of benefit.

PERSONAL YEAR 4: HARVESTING OPPORTUNITIES

PERSONAL YEAR 4 SUMMARY: Year 4 is a year to finalize. The past three years may have felt a bit like a roller coaster. Trail blaze (1), go within (2), then back out to meet new people and experience new ideas (3). But now it's time to reap the rewards. In addition to your expected manifestations, realize that it's likely you unknowingly laid the groundwork for the surprise opportunities as well. Some experiences in Year 4 could be:

PERSONAL YEAR 4: HARVESTING OPPORTUNITIES

Year Theme: To reap the harvest (over the past three years).

Role: To take advantage of any opportunities (planned or surprised).

Best at (on good days): Finishing projects.

Challenges (on bad days): Prioritizing the many opportunities so not scattered.

F.I.P.S.S. (FINANCIAL, INTELLECTUAL, PHYSICAL, SOCIAL, SPIRITUAL):

F—Strong time to make sound investments in career and other financial endeavors.

I—Strong time to be detailed and organized and get into the nuts and bolts of learning.

P—Strong time to revisit physical body issues that haven't been addressed.

So—Strong time to focus on inner circle and functional outer circle.

Sp—Strong time to solidify your rituals and ceremonies and practice them.

PERSONAL YEAR 5: CONSTANT CHANGE
AND GOOD FORTUNE

PERSONAL YEAR 5 SUMMARY: So you've come off a year of opportunities now let's sprinkle on a little luck. The key is to think fast and be flexible (as our family often says, keep a little bend in your knees). There are times when you won't have a lot of time to make decisions. It's time to trust your intuition so that you receive the full benefits of your 5 Year. Don't look back and say, "I knew I should've…" Some experiences in Year 5 could be:

PERSONAL YEAR 5: CONSTANT CHANGE AND GOOD FORTUNE

Year Theme: To take every advantage of a lucky year.

Role: To optimistically ride the wave of constant opportunities.

Best at (on good days): Being quick, raising to next level utilizing intuitive reflexes.

Challenges (on bad days): Being still. Not productive to use old learning for new opportunities.

F.I.P.S.S. (FINANCIAL, INTELLECTUAL, PHYSICAL, SOCIAL, SPIRITUAL):

F—Strong time to change jobs, careers, investment strategies.

I—Strong time to consider new learning paths and processes, particularly through travel.

P—Strong time to consistently move your physical body and be fit for the opportunities that arise.

So—Strong time to keep flexible relationships as you move forward (could also include physically moving).

Sp—Strong time to add flexibility in your rituals and ceremonies, maybe new information.

PERSONAL YEAR 6: BALANCING PERSONAL GROWTH AND RELATIONSHIPS

PERSONAL YEAR 6 SUMMARY: You have had two prior years of opportunities, and it's now time to go back inside. Inner circle relationships and personal development will be the prevailing energy for the year. This can be a difficult balance because you may be in demand in regards to your inner circle while you are in contemplation of your direction and growth. Reconsiderations are abundant and this is a staging energy for you to go deeper within yourself next year. Some experiences in Year 6 could be:

PERSONAL YEAR 6: BALANCING PERSONAL GROWTH AND RELATIONSHIPS

Year Theme: To achieve harmony and balance in all you hold dear.

Role: To be caregiver, comforter and become established in a "community(s)" (work, social, non-profit organizations…).

Best at (on good days): Empathizing. Renewal. Birthing.

Challenges (on bad days): Outer circle social events.

F.I.P.S.S. (FINANCIAL, INTELLECTUAL, PHYSICAL, SOCIAL, SPIRITUAL):

F—Strong time to reconsider or change jobs, careers, investment strategies.

I—Strong time to observe through life experiences, allow intuition to guide.

P—Strong time to consistently move your physical body, being conscious of not overdoing.

So—Strong time to focus on inner circle.

Sp—Strong time to go within to achieve harmony and balance.

PERSONAL YEAR 7: SOLITUDE AND REST

PERSONAL YEAR 7 SUMMARY: As you transition into this year the need to withdraw becomes stronger, to go deep within yourself. This is tough for your inner and outer circle relationships to understand. They may take it personally (you don't care about them, you're being selfish...). It would be a good idea to gently explain your path for the year to maintain your relationships in the future (even if you don't care about them right now). Make no mistake about it, you need this alone time. Embrace it. Some experiences in Year 7 could be:

PERSONAL YEAR 7: SOLITUDE AND REST

Year Theme: Inner Growth and Reflection.

Role: To focus on you.

Best at (on good days): Reading, rest and relaxation.

Challenges (on bad days): Any type of social activity or interaction outside of self.

F.I.P.S.S. (FINANCIAL, INTELLECTUAL, PHYSICAL, SOCIAL, SPIRITUAL):

F—Strong time not to make major changes to jobs, careers, investment strategies.

I—Strong time to study inwardly.

P—Strong time to methodically move your physical body with the added intention of enhancing inward experiences.

So—Strong time to be alone (can be awkward for even social Birth Mixes if not enough alone time).

Sp—Strong time to be on your own and making rituals and ceremonies that fit personal needs.

PERSONAL YEAR 8: MATERIAL REWARDS

PERSONAL YEAR 8 SUMMARY: 8 is the symbol of infinity and another harvest year. There are two harvest years in the nine year cycle—4 and 8. It's time to get physical and apply all your managerial skills to get there. All the rest that you experienced last year will be used as fuel for this year. Remember, however, that this is a good year to reap physical benefits but equally a time to experience loss if it is not managed effectively. Don't get too cocky. Some experiences in Year 8 could be:

PERSONAL YEAR 8: MATERIAL REWARDS

Year Theme: To harvest (what built over past seven years).

Role: To take advantage of earned opportunities.

Best at (on good days): Being efficient, focused and intuitive.

Challenges (on bad days): Allowing for rest.

F.I.P.S.S. (FINANCIAL, INTELLECTUAL, PHYSICAL, SOCIAL, SPIRITUAL):

F—Strong time to receive all material rewards or, if not careful, losses are experienced.

I—Strong time to execute your vision and experience physical rewards as opposed to studying or visualizing it.

P— Strong time to focus on keeping your physical body fit.

So—Strong time to focus on your ability to maximize manifesting this year and may not include as many inner or outer circle interactions.

Sp—Strong time to independently practice your rituals and ceremonies and make quality time count.

PERSONAL YEAR 9: CLUTTER CLEARING

PERSONAL YEAR 9 SUMMARY: So now you're in the last year of this cycle. You've reflected, rebirthed, pursued, and harvested over the past eight years and now it's time to purge physical and spiritual junk that isn't serving you after all your trial and errors. Next year is the beginning of a brand new nine year cycle. Take a deep breath after every purge because there will be many (or, at least, this is what the energy supports). Congratulate yourself after every cosmic confrontation and remind yourself how far you have come. Some experiences in Year 9 could be:

PERSONAL YEAR 9: CLUTTER CLEARING

Year Theme: To purge life ideas or items that hold you back in any way.

Role: Soul Clutter buster.

Best at (on good days): Preparing, confronting, completion.

Challenges (on bad days): Moving backwards due to fear of letting go.

F.I.P.S.S. (FINANCIAL, INTELLECTUAL, PHYSICAL, SOCIAL, SPIRITUAL):

F—Strong time to purge things in jobs, careers, investment strategies that don't serve higher purpose.

I—Strong time to remove obstacles from new learning paths and processes.

P—Strong time to remove all bad habits connected to your physical body.

So—Strong time to purge relationships that hold you back and adopt positive patterns.

Sp—Strong time to purge old rituals and ceremonies that don't serve your highest good.

About the Author

Michelle Payton helps others simplify all areas of their lives through conscious living and confidence building communication. She provides information that gives people full access to soul-based happiness.

She has attracted all good things into her and others lives as a multiple award-winning author, publishing *Adventures of a Mainstream Metaphysical Mom*, *"Soul"utions, Birth Mix Patterns: Astrology, Numerology, and Birth Order, and their effects on the Past, Present, and Future*, *Birth Mix Patterns: for Families, and Other Groups that Matter* and now *Birth Mix Patterns and Loving Relationships Using Astrology, Numerology, and Birth Order*

She helps people to work from their heart centers as Now Age parents, partners, professionals, and individuals beginning with a Bachelor's degree in Communication Arts, as a Birth Mix Patterns Master, as a PhD candidate in Hypnotherapy, and as a Master Neuro-linguistic Programmer™. She touches people world-wide as a regular radio guest and as a writer for numerous regional and national publications. She offers empowering one-on-one sessions, on-site and tele(phone)-seminars world-wide (business-to-business and consumer). Her many offerings can be found at www.MichellePayton.com and www.HelpingUExpand.com.

She is also the founder and owner of an international wholesale cooperative wholesale distributorship called The Left Side (www.TheLeftSide.com). Known for its thousands of quality body, mind, spirit focused brands, products, and services, Michelle's books can be purchased wholesale from this organization.

In addition to her mainstream metaphysical personal and professional path, Michelle has been an accomplished national consumer brand marketer for more than 20 years resulting in an extensive advertising, marketing, research, writing, speaking, and business building background. She, her husband and life partner since 1982, and three children currently reside in Columbus, Ohio.

For more information on Michelle's products and services visit:

www.TheLeftSide.com – for wholesale purchases

www.MichellePayton.com – for retail purchases, one-on-one sessions, on-site, and tele(phone)-education and Books Clubs

www.HelpingUExpand.com – tele(phone)-seminars of masters in soul-based living

Call: 614-785-9821

Emails: TheLeftSide@aol.com, MAMichellePayton@gmail.com, HelpingUExpand@gmail.com

About Michelle's Books

Mainstream Metaphysical Living

As a conscious living and confidence building communicator, Michelle's work gives tips on how to accomplish 21st century, soul-based living as a mainstream metaphysical parent, partner, professional, and individual, and how this has unfolded throughout history.

Adventures of a Mainstream Metaphysical Mom: Choosing Peace of Mind in a World of Diverse Ideas

Mainstream Metaphysical Parenting, Mentoring, and Relationships with self and others in the 21st Century!

2003 Finalist for Best Biographical/ Self-Help Book — Coalition of Visionary Resources, 2003 Visionary Award, International New Age Trade Show

192 pp ~ paperback
ISBN: 0-9719804-0-3
ISBN-13: 978-0-9719804-0-2

$13.95

"Soul"utions: Achieving Financial, Intellectual, Physical, Social, and Spiritual Balance with Soul

Tips on soul-based living using eye-opening goal setting principles in all areas of life!

239 pp ~ paperback
ISBN: 0-9719804-1-1
ISBN-13: 978-0-9719804-1-9
$14.95

Birth Mix Patterns: Astrology, Numerology, and Birth Order, and their effects on the Past, Present, and Future

Analyzes hundreds of historical figures, including United States Presidents and First Ladies, artists, authors, civil rights leaders, and more in connection with Astrology, Numerology, and Birth Order.

2006 Finalist for Best General Interest/How To Book — Coalition of Visionary Resources, 2006 Visionary Award, International New Age Trade Show

160 pp ~ paperback
ISBN: 0-9719804-2-x
ISBN-13: 978-0-9719804-2-6
$12.95

Birth Mix Patterns: Astrology, Numerology, and Birth Order, and their effects on Families & Other Groups that Matter

Analyzes the authors of the Declaration of Independence, Dark Leaders, the Supreme Court Justices, the Beatles and more in connection with Astrology, Numerology, and Birth Order.

133 pp ~ paperback

ISBN-10: 0-9719804-3-8

ISBN–13: 978-0-9719804-3-3

$12.95

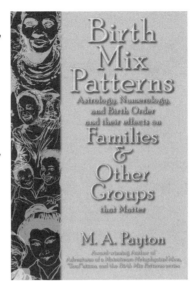

Index

Beckham, Victoria Caroline (Posh) .5, 20, 21, 23
Born: April 17, 1974
Birth Order/Siblings: First Born (of three children)
http://en.wikipedia.org/wiki/Victoria_Beckham
http://www.imdb.com/name/nm0065751/
http://en.wikipedia.org/wiki/Spice_Girls

Beckham, David 5, 20, 21, 22, 23
Born: May 2, 1975
Birth Order/Siblings:
http://en.wikipedia.org/wiki/David_Beckham
http://www.beckham-magazine.com/frames.html
http://www.ocduk.org/1/ocd.htm
http://news.independent.co.uk/uk/health_medical/article355701.ece

Bono, Sonny. 5, 23, 24, 26
Born: February 16, 1935
Birth Order/Siblings: Unknown
http://en.wikipedia.org/wiki/Sonny_Bono
http://www.imdb.com/name/nm0095122/
http://www.classicbands.com/sonnycher.html

Burton, Richard. 5, 17, 18, 19, 20
Born: November 10, 1945
Birth Order/Siblings: Unknown, reports of many brothers and sisters
http://en.wikipedia.org/wiki/Richard_Burton
http://www.richardburton.com/home.htm

Born: May 20, 1946
Birth Order/Siblings: Unknown, reports of one younger sister with age difference unknown
http://hb.syl.com/cherthisisanamethateveryoneknows.html
http://www.cher.com
http://en.wikipedia.org/wiki/Cher

Born: August 24, 1964
Birth Order/Siblings: Unknown
http://en.wikipedia.org/wiki/Julie_Cypher

Born: January 26, 1958
Birth Order/Siblings: First Born Girl (one brother 4 years age difference)
http://en.wikipedia.org/wiki/Ellen_DeGeneres
http://www.imdb.com/name/nm0001122/
http://www.ellen-degeneres.com/

Born: January 31, 1973
Birth Order/Siblings: Unknown
http://en.wikipedia.org/wiki/Portia_de_Rossi
http://imdb.com/name/nm0005577/
http://lesbianlife.about.com/od/lesbianactors/p/PortiadeRossi.htm

Jolie, Angelina 5, 27, 32, 33
Born: June 4, 1975
Birth Order/Siblings: First Born girl, one brother
Sources: www.imdb.com/name/nm0001401/, http://en.wikipedia.org/
wiki/Angelina_Jolie
www.superiorpics.com/angelina_jolie/

King, Coretta Scott 5, 36, 37, 39
Born: April 27, 1927
Birth Order/Siblings: Unknown, reports of younger brother, older sister
www.who2.com/corettascottking.html
http://www.stanford.edu/group/King/about_king/details/270427b.
htm
http://www2.lhric.org/pocantico/womenenc/king3.htm

King Jr., Martin Luther 5, 36, 38, 39
Born: January 15, 1929
Birth Order/Siblings: Middle boy, two brothers—one older, one younger
http://en.wikipedia.org/wiki/Martin_Luther_King,_Jr.
http://www.mccsc.edu/~kmcglaun/mlk/bio.htm

Born: March 28, 1970
Birth Order/Siblings: First Born boy (two older sisters, unsure age difference which could indicate Only)
Sources: http://en.wikipedia.org/wiki/Vince_Vaughn, www.imdb.com/name/nmooooo681/
www.vincev.com/bio.html

Born: July 17, 1947
Birth Order/Siblings: First Born Girl (one younger sister, one younger brother)
http://en.wikipedia.org/wiki/Camilla%2C_The_Duchess_of_Cornwall
http://www.who2.com/camillaparkerbowles.html
http://www.theroyalist.net/content/view/823/40/

Born: November 14, 1948
Birth Order/Siblings: First Born Boy
http://www.who2.com/charlesprinceofwales.html
http://en.wikipedia.org/wiki/Charles%2C_Prince_of_Wales

Born: January 29, 1954

Birth Order/Siblings: Only

http://en.wikipedia.org/wiki/Oprah_Winfrey

http://www2.oprah.com/index.jhtml

http://www.oprah.com

Notes

Notes

Notes

Notes

Notes